Gooseberry Patch co.

A Country Store In Your Mailbox®

A Pinch of This, A Dash of That

A Country Store In Your Mailbox®

Gooseberry Patch
600 London Road
Department Book
Delaware, OH 43015

1-800-854-6673
gooseberrypatch.com

Copyright 1998, Gooseberry Patch® 1-888052-33-3
Seventh Printing, July, 2002

How To Subscribe

Would you like to receive
"A Country Store in Your Mailbox"®?
For a 2-year subscription to our 96-page
Gooseberry Patch catalog, simply send $3.00 to:

Gooseberry Patch
600 London Road
Delaware, OH 43015

Contents

DEDICATION

For everyone who celebrates the sweet memories of Grandma's cooking.

APPRECIATION

Thanks to our wonderful friends, for sharing your heart-felt memories and favorite recipes!

Farmhouse
Breakfasts

Growing up, my sister and I spent many weekends at our grandparents' farm...wintry Saturday mornings were always our favorite! While we were still warmly tucked under several quilts, Grandpa was up early on those frosty mornings feeding animals and milking cows. Up just as early, Grandma could be found puttering in the kitchen and before long we would wake up to the smell of sizzling sausage and fresh coffee.

We'd quickly dress and run downstairs to be greeted by a table set with biscuits, sausage gravy, home fries, eggs and homemade bread with fresh butter! We always ate a hearty breakfast; Grandpa said we needed it to give us energy for the day's chores.

Now, many years later, my family enjoys the same hearty breakfast on chilly Saturday mornings. As I listen to the gusty wind whistling through the pines, I realize we never outgrow our need for simplicity and family traditions.

Buttermilk-Chocolate Muffins

Marion Herman
Topeka, KS

Stir in some chocolate or peanut butter chips for variety.

1-3/4 c. flour
3 T. unsweetened cocoa powder
3 T. brown sugar, firmly packed
3 T. sugar
2-1/2 t. baking powder

1/2 t. baking soda
1/2 t. salt
1 c. buttermilk
2 lg. eggs

Mix all dry ingredients together. In a separate bowl, combine buttermilk and eggs. Make a well in the center of dry ingredients and pour in the egg and buttermilk mixture. Mix until just moistened. Spoon into muffin pan and bake at 400 degrees for 15 minutes.

A collection of old buttons or spools will look great in one of Grandma's glass canning jars. Try to find jars with tin or zinc lids for a real old-fashioned feel.

Grammy Irene's Sticky Buns

Cindy Johnston-Bumar
Loyalhanna, PA

I remember my sister and I standing with our mouths watering when Mom would make these. Eat them warm from the oven; there's nothing better!

1/3 c. milk
1/4 c. sugar
1/2 t. salt
1/4 c. butter
1 pkg. active dry yeast

1/4 c. warm water
1 egg
2-1/2 c. all-purpose flour, divided

In a small pan, heat milk until bubbles form around edge of pan. Remove from heat. Add sugar, salt and butter. Stir to melt, cool to lukewarm. Sprinkle yeast over water in large bowl. Stir to dissolve. Stir in lukewarm milk mixture. Add the egg and 2 cups of flour. Beat with electric mixer until smooth. Add remaining 1/2 cup of flour and mix by hand until dough is smooth and leaves the sides of the bowl. Turn dough onto lightly floured pastry cloth. Knead until dough is smooth and blisters appear. Place in a lightly greased large bowl, turning to bring greased side up. Cover with towel. Let rise in a warm place, free from drafts until double in size, about one to 1-1/2 hours.

Filling:

1/2 c. butter, softened and
   divided
1 c. brown sugar, divided

1/2 c. pecans or walnut halves
1/2 c. raisins
1/2 t. ground cinnamon

Cream 1/4 cup butter and 1/2 cup brown sugar. Spread on bottom and sides of 9"x9"x2" pan. Sprinkle butter mixture with nuts. Roll dough on lightly floured surface into a 16"x12" rectangle. Spread with remaining butter and brown sugar. Sprinkle on raisins and cinnamon. Roll up long side, pinching edges to seal. Cut crosswise into 12 slices and place cut side down in pan. Let rise, covered, in a warm place until doubled. Bake at 375 degrees for 30 minutes or until golden. Invert on board, let stand for one minute then remove from pan. Makes 12 rolls.

Popover Pancake

Karen Pilcher
Burleson, TX

Enjoy this extra large puffy pancake with a hot mug of tea.

1/2 c. flour
1/2 c. milk
2 eggs

1/4 c. butter
2 t. powdered sugar
juice of half a lemon

In a mixing bowl, beat together flour, milk and eggs until slightly lumpy. Melt butter in a 9"x9" pan and then pour in the batter. Bake at 350 degrees for 20 minutes until puffy. Sprinkle powdered sugar and lemon juice over the pancake, and return to oven for 2 to 3 minutes.

Old berry pails are beautiful filled to the brim with rosehips; you can even tuck a votive inside!

Apple Fritters

Joanne West
Beavercreek, OH

An Ohio favorite!

1 c. flour
1-1/2 t. baking powder
2 T. sugar
1/2 t. salt

1 egg, beaten
1/2 c. plus 1 T. milk
1-1/2 c. apples, pared and diced
vegetable oil

Sift dry ingredients together. Combine egg and milk. Pour into dry ingredients and stir until batter is smooth. Add apples to batter and blend well. Add enough oil to equal one inch deep in a heavy skillet. Drop batter by spoonfuls in hot oil and fry until golden brown on both sides. For a quicker version, core and slice the apples in rings, dip in batter and fry until golden.

Enjoy the little things, for one day you may look back and realize they were the big things.

—Robert Brault

Farmhouse Breakfasts

Orange Breakfast Crescents

Teresa Sullivan
Westerville, OH

Enjoy these warm while the icing is still melting!

3 oz. cream cheese
3 T. sugar
1/4 t. almond extract

1 t. orange zest, grated
1 pkg. 8-count refrigerated
   crescent rolls

Blend first 4 ingredients. Separate dough into triangles. Divide cheese mixture among dough triangles, spread, leaving a 1/4-inch border. Roll each, starting at the long edge. Place on lightly greased cookie sheet, shaping into crescents. Bake at 350 degrees for 15 minutes or until lightly browned.

Topping:

1/2 c. powdered sugar
1 T. orange juice
1 t. orange zest, grated

1 t. margarine, melted
1/8 t. almond extract

Combine all ingredients while rolls are baking. Spread over hot crescent rolls and serve immediately.

Antique quilts that are torn, can still be used! They make wonderful table runners, doll quilts or Christmas tree skirts.

Sweetheart Muffins

Kimberly McDole
Sparta, NJ

Make someone you love feel special...serve these muffins in a basket lined with an embroidered handkerchief.

6 T. butter
3/4 c. sugar
2 eggs
1/2 c. milk
2 c. strawberries, rinsed and
    stems removed

2 c. all-purpose flour
1/4 t. salt
1 T. baking powder
milk chocolate drops or your
    favorite flavor of jam

Preheat oven to 350 degrees. In a large bowl, cream together butter and sugar. Mix in the eggs, one at a time and add the milk. Mash the berries or purée in blender. Stir the berries into the butter and milk mixture. In a separate bowl, sift the flour, salt and baking powder. Stir well. Add the flour mixture to the berry mixture. Use a wooden spoon to stir. Line the muffin tin with paper liners. Drop the batter from a tablespoon to fill the cups halfway. Add a sweet surprise: a milk chocolate drop, or 1/2 teaspoon of jam. Then spoon more batter and fill almost to the top. Bake until the muffins begin to brown and a toothpick inserted near the center comes out clean, about 20 to 25 minutes. Remove muffins from tin and cool. Makes 12 muffins.

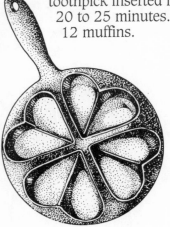

All happiness depends on a leisurely breakfast.

—John Gunther

Amish Sweet Rolls   *Jo Ann*

Best with an icy cold glass of milk!

1 pkg. active dry yeast
1/4 c. warm water
1/4 c. plus 1 T. shortening, divided
1/4 c. sugar

1 c. milk, scalded or 1 c. water
1 t. salt
3-1/4 to 4 c. flour
1 egg, beaten

Dissolve yeast in warm water. In a large bowl, combine 1/4 cup shortening and sugar. Pour hot milk or water over mixture. Cool to lukewarm. Blend salt into flour. Add one cup of flour to sugar mixture and beat well. Beat in yeast mixture and egg. Gradually add remaining flour to form soft dough, beating well. Brush top of dough with 1 tablespoon softened shortening. Cover and let rise in warm place until doubled, about one to 2 hours. Punch down and knead. Divide dough in half. Roll each half into a rectangle approximately 12"x8".

Filling:

1/4 c. butter
1/2 c. brown sugar

1 t. cinnamon

Spread each section of dough with butter. Combine brown sugar and cinnamon and sprinkle over butter. Roll dough from long side. Cut into 1-1/2 inch slices. Place rolls in greased pans about 3/4 inches apart. Let rise and bake at 350 degrees for 30 minutes. Cool to warm. Frost with your favorite powdered sugar icing recipe if desired. Makes 2 dozen rolls.

To have grown wise and kind is real success.
-Anonymous

Cinnamon Flop

Donna Dye
Ray, OH

A favorite recipe found in an old Amish cookbook.

1 c. sugar
2 c. flour
2 t. baking powder
1 T. butter, melted

1 c. milk
brown sugar
cinnamon
butter

Sift sugar, flour and baking powder together. Add butter and milk and stir until well blended. Divide mixture between 2 well-oiled 9" pie or cake pans. Sprinkle dough with desired amounts of brown sugar and cinnamon, and add pats of butter. Bake at 350 degrees for 30 minutes.

When I was a little girl, I always wanted to be in the kitchen, because it was warm, and that's where my mother was. You never lose that feeling.

-Dolly Parton

Farmhouse Breakfasts

Flaky Date Scones

*The Governor's Inn
Ludlow, VT*

Enjoy these topped with homemade preserves or sweet cream butter.

1-1/4 c. flour
2-1/2 t. baking powder
1/2 t. salt
2 T. sugar

6 T. sweet butter, unsalted
2 lg. eggs, beaten
1/3 c. milk
1/2 c. pitted dates, chopped

Mix flour, baking powder, salt, one tablespoon sugar and butter until mixture resembles crumbs. Beat eggs and reserve one tablespoonful. Add milk, dates and eggs to flour mixture; stir until dough is formed. Roll dough on lightly floured surface into 9"x6" rectangle about 1/2-inch thick. Cut into 3-inch squares and then into triangles. Place these about an inch apart on a greased cookie sheet. Brush with reserved egg and sprinkle with one tablespoon sugar. Bake at 350 degrees for 12 minutes until golden brown. Serves 12.

Egg cups from the 1950's make delicate vases for springtime tulips or daffodils.

Sugar-Nut Coffeecake

Eleanor Bierley
Miamisburg, OH

This coffeecake is filled with sweet layers of sugar and nuts!

3 eggs
1/2 c. margarine
3/4 c. sugar
1 T. vanilla

2 c. flour
1 t. baking powder
1 c. sour cream

Lightly oil a Bundt® pan, set aside. In a medium bowl, cream together eggs and margarine. Blend in sugar and vanilla. Sift together flour and baking powder, add to egg mixture. Fold in sour cream. Set aside to prepare sugar-nut mixture.

Sugar-Nut Mixture:

1 c. brown sugar
1 c. nuts, chopped

6 T. butter
2 t. cinnamon

Combine all ingredients in a small bowl. Spread half the coffeecake batter in Bundt® pan; sprinkle sugar-nut mixture evenly over top. Spoon on the remaining batter and gently spread to cover filling. Bake at 350 degrees for 30 minutes. Drizzle with powdered sugar icing if desired.

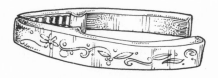

It isn't so much what's on the table that matters, as what's on the chairs.

-W. S. Gilbert

Blueberry Coffeecake

Susan Kennedy
Delaware, OH

A very moist coffeecake; bursting with fresh berry flavor!

2 c. flour
1 c. sugar
3 t. baking powder
1 t. salt

1/3 c. margarine, softened
1 c. milk
1 egg
1 c. blueberries

Preheat oven to 350 degrees. Beat all ingredients, except blueberries, in a large bowl on a low speed for 30 seconds. Then beat on a medium speed for 2 minutes, scraping bowl occasionally. Grease a 13"x9" pan. Spread half the batter in the pan. Sprinkle one cup of blueberries over batter, then top with the rest of batter. Add streusel topping below, then bake in oven for 40 minutes.

Streusel:

1/2 c. walnuts, chopped
1/3 c. brown sugar
1/4 c. flour

1/2 t. cinnamon
3 t. margarine

Mix all ingredients together until crumbly. Sprinkle on top of cake.

Glaze:

1 c. powdered sugar
2 T. milk
1/4 t. vanilla extract

Combine all ingredients, drizzle over top of coffeecake.

Apple-Stuffed French Toast

Marie Stutz
Denver, PA

It's long been a family tradition that on Sundays, our family attends church services together and then comes home to a yummy brunch. Since we love to eat breakfast, but have little time for it during the week, we make our Sunday gatherings an event. This is one of our favorites.

12 slices bread
20-oz. can apple pie filling
1/4 c. pecan meal
cinnamon

10 eggs
1/2 c. milk
1 t. vanilla

Oil a 13"x10" baking dish. Place 6 slices of bread on the bottom of the dish, add a tablespoon of apple pie filling on top of each slice. Sprinkle pie filling with pecan meal, which can be found in the bulk food section of your grocery store, and cinnamon. Place the remaining 6 slices over the pie filling. Beat eggs, milk and vanilla together; pour over bread slices. Refrigerate overnight. Prepare crumb topping before baking.

Crumb Topping:

1/4 c. butter
1/4 c. brown sugar
1/4 c. pecan meal

1/2 c. oatmeal
1/4 c. flour
2 t. cinnamon

Combine all ingredients and sprinkle over bread slices. Bake at 350 degrees for 35 to 45 minutes, or until eggs are set.

Wrap a small twig wreath around homespun napkins!

Coffee Mug Bread

Vickie

This will be a new favorite!

1 T. cinnamon
1/2 c. sugar
2 T. walnuts, chopped

1 loaf frozen bread dough
Garnish: cinnamon sticks

In a medium-size bowl, combine cinnamon, sugar and walnuts. Oil the insides of 2 coffee mugs. Partially thaw a loaf of frozen bread dough. Cut the loaf in half crosswise. Then divide each half into 4 strips. Roll each strip between the palms of your hands, and then dredge it in a mixture of cinnamon, sugar and walnuts. Twist 2 strips together, divide in half, and place each half in a spiral fashion into 2 mugs. Let the dough rise until double in bulk. The dough will extend beyond the top of the mug and resemble a swirl of whipped cream topping. Bake about 15 minutes in a 350 degree oven. Garnish with a cinnamon stick, and serve immediately in the mug. Repeat with remaining dough. Serves 8.

Animal crackers and cocoa to drink. That is the finest of suppers, I think. When I'm grown up and can have what I please, I think I shall always insist upon these.

— Christopher Morley

Country Cheese Omelet

Helen Murray
Piketon, OH

Make this a hearty country breakfast and serve with hashbrowns, biscuits and sausage!

3 eggs, room temperature
1 T. milk
1/4 t. salt
1/4 t. black pepper

1 T. butter
1/4 c. Cheddar cheese, finely
  shredded

In a medium-size bowl, whisk together eggs, milk, salt and pepper. In an 8" skillet or omelet pan, melt butter over low heat until foamy but not browned. Increase the heat to moderately high and tip the pan to coat with butter. Pour in egg mixture. As the omelet cooks, tilt the pan and draw the edges in toward the center with a fork. Shake pan gently to distribute the uncooked portion. When the omelet is just set, about 2 minutes, remove from the heat and sprinkle with cheese. Loosen the edges of the omelet with a fork and as you tip the pan forward to fold the omelet in half, slide the omelet onto a warmed serving plate. Makes one serving.

Nothing is quite as intoxicating as the smell of bacon frying in the morning, save perhaps the smell of coffee brewing.

-James Beard

Farmhouse Breakfasts

Farmhouse Sausage Gravy

Ann Magner
New Port Richey, FL

Create a homestyle breakfast, serve over split buttermilk biscuits!

1/2 lb. mild or sweet sausage	3/4 c. milk
1/2 lb. spicy Italian sausage	3/4 c. chicken broth
3 T. flour	salt and pepper to taste

Cook sausage in a large non-stick skillet over medium-high heat until browned and cooked. Transfer sausage to a bowl, set aside. Remove all but 3 tablespoons of the fat from the skillet. Sprinkle flour into the skillet, stir well. Cook over medium-high heat for one minute, stirring constantly. Remove skillet from the heat and slowly add the milk and the broth. Whisk mixture until completely smooth. Return skillet to the stove and cook until the gravy is slightly thickened. Salt and pepper to taste, add the crumbled sausage and combine well. Continue to cook over medium heat until thoroughly heated. Serves 6.

I came from a home
where gravy was
a beverage!

-Erma Bombeck

Rise 'n Shine Hash Browns

Sally Foor
Jeromesville, OH

If you want to add a little more flavor to your hash browns, add chopped green pepper and onion to taste.

2 potatoes, peeled
salt and pepper to taste

1 T. vegetable oil
1 T. unsalted butter

Grate potatoes into a medium-size bowl and season with salt and pepper. In a non-stick skillet, heat oil and butter over medium heat. Add grated potatoes, pat them down to form a pancake. Cover the skillet and cook potatoes until browned on the bottom. Turn potato pancake over and cook 10 minutes longer or until browned. Cut into 4 wedges.

Look for old seed packets at yard sales...they look terrific tucked in cupboard door panels or indoor shutters!

Farmhouse Breakfasts

Bacon-Cheddar Cups

Laura Fenneman
Lima, OH

Perfect for a family breakfast buffet...they'll go fast!

12 slices white bread
1 T. butter
4 slices bacon, crisply cooked
    and crumbled
1 egg, beaten
1/2 c. whipping cream

1/2 T. chives
1/2 T. onion powder
1/2 c. Cheddar cheese, shredded
salt and pepper to taste
Garnish: cherry tomatoes,
    mushrooms

Cut a 3-inch circle from center of each slice of bread. Roll out each circle with rolling pin to flatten slightly. Grease a 12-cup muffin tin with butter. Press one bread circle in each pan to form a cup. Bake in a 350 degree oven for 7 minutes. Divide bacon among cups. Combine egg, whipping cream, chives, onion powder and divide among cups. Sprinkle with cheese. Bake in a 350 degree oven for 12 minutes. Let stand 5 minutes before removing to plate. Garnish with cherry tomatoes or mushrooms.

Cheese...milk's leap toward immortality.

-Clifton Fadiman

Brown Sugar French Toast

Cherie Shortway
Sussex, NJ

Serve warm from the oven...delicious and so easy!

1 c. brown sugar, packed
1/2 c. butter
2 T. light corn syrup
1 loaf French bread, cut into
    1-inch slices

5 eggs
1-1/2 c. milk
1 t. vanilla

Place first 3 ingredients in medium-size saucepan and heat over medium heat. Spray 13"x9" baking dish with non-stick vegetable oil. Pour hot mixture into baking dish. Place sliced bread over mixture and push bread slices closely together. Beat eggs; add milk and vanilla and mix slightly. Pour egg mixture over bread, covering each slice well. Cover the baking dish with plastic wrap and refrigerate overnight. The next morning, preheat oven to 350 degrees and place uncovered dish in oven for 30 minutes. Serve directly from baking dish or turn onto plates.

Oh, it's nice to get up on the mornin', but it's nicer to lie in bed.

-Sir Harry Lauder

Farmhouse Breakfasts

Garden-Fresh Denver Omelet

Donna Dye
Ray, OH

You can add any of your favorite vegetables, fresh from the garden!

1 slice of bacon, cut into
    1/2-inch pieces
2 T. red bell pepper, diced
2 T. green bell pepper, diced
2 T. red onion, diced
1 slice baked ham, shredded

2 lg. eggs
1/4 c. milk
salt and pepper to taste
1 t. fresh chives
2 t. unsalted butter
Garnish: sour cream and salsa

Place the bacon in a non-stick skillet and cook over medium-low heat until just crisp, 5 minutes. Using a slotted spoon, transfer the bacon to a paper towel to drain. Remove and discard all but one tablespoon of the bacon fat. Add both the peppers and the onion to the skillet and cook over low heat, stirring until just wilted, about 5 minutes. Transfer the vegetables to a bowl and add the bacon and ham. In a separate bowl, beat the eggs with the milk. Season with salt and pepper and whisk in the chives. Stir in the vegetable mixture. Melt the butter in a non-stick skillet over medium heat until it foams. Add the egg mixture and cook without stirring until the omelet begins to set around the edges. Using a fork, push the set eggs into the center letting the uncooked eggs run out to the edges. Continue cooking, making sure the filling is distributed evenly. Cover the pan with a lid and cook for 30 to 45 seconds more, or until the eggs are cooked to the desired doneness. Slide the omelet halfway onto a plate, then flip it over itself. Serve with sour cream and salsa.

Love and eggs are best when they are fresh.

-Russian saying

Early Riser Home Fries

Becky Sykes
Gooseberry Patch

Serve these crispy potatoes with eggs and sausage on the side!

4 russet potatoes
1/4 c. oil
1 lg. green bell pepper, seeded
   and chopped

1 lg. onion, chopped
salt and pepper to taste

Wash potatoes, pat dry, and prick with the tines of a fork. Bake potatoes at 375 degrees for one hour. When potatoes have cooled slightly, cut them into one-inch pieces. Heat the oil in a large non-stick skillet over medium heat and add the bell pepper and onion. Cook until lightly browned, about 10 minutes. Add the potatoes to the skillet and stir well. Salt and pepper to taste. Continue to cook potatoes 10 minutes, or until crispy and lightly browned, turning occasionally with a spatula. Serves 4 to 6.

Nothing helps scenery like ham and eggs.

-Mark Twain

Old-fashioned Breads

As kids we always came home through the kitchen door. Just outside was a woodpile stacked high, kindling in a brass bucket and the scent of woodsmoke in the air. We'd stop just long enough to take off muddy boots or wet shoes, Mom's rule, and then run inside! It was our favorite place because Mom could be found there.

One of our best memories is the aroma of bread baking in the oven...we could hardly wait to have some; still warm with lots of butter! We'd sink our teeth into a thick slice, gobble it up and ask for another! Sometimes we topped it with homemade jam and we always had a glass of icy cold milk!

Even today, the smell of freshly baked bread takes me back to those days.

Old-fashioned Breads

The Best Bread in the World

Ann Marie Pastore
Powell, OH

Very easy to make and such a treat when the butter melts instantly on a still warm slice.

2 c. boiling water
1 c. rolled oats, uncooked
1/3 c. lukewarm water
2 pkgs. active dry yeast
1 T. salt
1/2 c. honey

2 T. butter, melted and cooled
2-1/2 to 3 c. unbleached flour
1-1/2 to 2 c. whole wheat flour
1 egg yolk
1 T. water
sesame seeds

Pour water over oats. Let stand until thoroughly softened. Soak yeast in lukewarm water. Add the salt, honey and melted butter to the oats. Making sure the oats are lukewarm, add the yeast and mix well. Gradually add the flours and knead with your hands about 5 minutes. Put dough into lightly oiled bowl, turning it around to coat dough on all sides. Cover with a cloth and let rise for one hour or until doubled. Oil, or spray 2 bread tins or cookie sheets. Punch down the risen bread dough and cut in half. Knead each half briefly and shape into loaves, a braid or round loaves. Place dough on a cookie sheet and preheat oven to 350 degrees. Beat egg yolk with water and brush surface of each loaf, sprinkle with sesame seeds. Bake for 35 to 40 minutes. Turn the loaves onto a rack and let cool.

Use your summer herbs to make beautiful wreaths. Sage and Sweet Annie are long-lasting and fragrant!

Sour Cream Corn Muffins

Kathy Moberg
Saline, MI

Serve warm with a bowl of chili or vegetable soup.

1 c. yellow cornmeal
1 c. flour
1/4 c. sugar
2 t. baking powder
1 t. salt

1/2 t. baking soda
1 c. sour cream
2 lg. eggs
1/4 c. butter, melted

Grease muffin tin well and preheat oven to 425 degrees. In a large bowl, combine cornmeal, flour, sugar, baking powder, salt and baking soda. Mix together. In a small bowl, combine sour cream, eggs, and butter. Mix thoroughly. Then add to dry ingredients. Stir until moistened. Spoon batter into 12-cup muffin tin and bake at 425 degrees for 15 to 20 minutes, until golden brown.

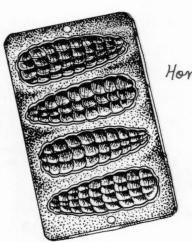

Honest bread is very well...it's
the butter that makes
the temptation.

-Douglas William Jerrold

Old-fashioned Breads

Feather Bed Rolls

Liz Kenneweg
Gooseberry Patch

This recipe comes from a very old family cookbook my mother had...it's listed under the section, "Foods Men Rave About!"

1 cake compressed yeast
2-1/2 c. milk
1/2 c. shortening

2 T. sugar
2 t. salt
5 c. flour

Crumble yeast into a bowl. Scald milk and cool to 80 degrees. Add to yeast. Cream shortening and sugar together. Add salt and the yeast-milk mixture. Sift flour once before measuring. Add flour to above mixture and beat with a spoon until smooth. Allow to rise until double in bulk, about one hour. Place a spoonful of dough into each greased muffin cup filling 2/3 full. Let rise again until double in bulk, 20 to 30 minutes. Bake until golden brown. Bake at 425 degrees for 20 minutes or until golden brown. Brush rolls with butter after removing them from the oven. Makes 3 dozen rolls.

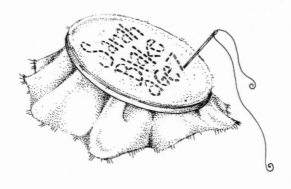

Jelly is a food usually found on bread, children and piano keys.

- Anonymous

Grandma's Special Potato Buns

Shirley Young
Jersey Shore, PA

This recipe brings back wonderful childhood memories of going to Grandma's house. As soon as we walked into her old farmhouse, we'd head for the out-kitchen to sample her bounty.

1 pkg. yeast
1 c. lukewarm water
1 c. mashed potatoes
2 eggs, beaten

1/2 c. shortening
1/2 c. sugar
1 t. salt
3-1/2 c. flour

Dissolve yeast in water. Combine with potatoes, eggs, shortening, sugar and salt. Mix well. Blend in flour. Place dough in an oiled bowl, turning once to coat. Let dough rise for 2 hours. Roll out to 1/2-inch thick and cut with a biscuit cutter. Let rise. Rub butter on tops and sprinkle lightly with sugar. Bake at 400 degrees for 7 minutes or until tops begin to brown.

Bread is like dresses, hats and shoes...
in other words, essential!

-Emily Post

Poppy Seed Bread

Linda Thomas
Everett, WA

An old-fashioned sweet bread.

3 eggs
1-1/2 c. milk
1-1/8 c. vegetable oil
1-1/2 t. vanilla
1-1/2 t. almond extract
1-1/2 t. butter flavoring

2-1/3 c. sugar
2 T. poppy seeds
1-1/2 t. salt
1/2 t. baking powder
3 c. flour

Beat eggs together in a large mixing bowl and add all liquid ingredients. Mix well and then add dry ingredients. Pour into 2 lightly greased loaf pans and bake at 325 degrees for one hour. Let cool for 10 minutes in pans.

Glaze:

1/4 c. orange juice
1/2 c. sugar
1/2 t. vanilla

1/2 t. almond extract
1/2 t. butter flavoring

Mix all ingredients together until sugar is dissolved completely. Pour glaze on top and leave in pans to cool completely.

What is a home without Mother?

-Alice Hawthorne

Apple-Nut Bread

Angie Stevens
South Point, OH

Serve this bread with an icy cold glass of milk...it makes a yummy after-school treat!

2 c. vegetable oil
1-1/2 c. sugar
3 eggs
1 t. vanilla
3 c. flour
1-1/2 t. baking soda
1/2 t. salt

1 t. cinnamon
1 t. nutmeg
1 t. clove
1 t. ginger
3 c. apples, chopped
1 c. nuts

Combine oil, sugar, eggs and vanilla in a mixing bowl and beat with an electric mixer. In separate bowl, mix together all dry ingredients. Add dry ingredients to oil and sugar mixture. Mix on low speed until blended. Stir in apples and nuts and mix well by hand. Pour batter into a greased and floured Bundt® pan and bake at 350 degrees for one hour and 15 minutes. Let cool in pan for 15 minutes before removing.

A child-size coffeepot is the perfect place to display your favorite coffee-scented candles!

Old-fashioned Breads

Loving Loaf

Sandy White
Long Beach, MS

An "upside down" loaf of bread!

Topping:

1/2 c. butter, melted
1/3 c. sugar

1-1/2 c. vanilla wafers, crushed
1 c. pecans, finely chopped

Combine topping ingredients. Mix thoroughly. Pat into bottom of 2 well-greased loaf pans. Set aside.

Batter:

1 c. butter
2 c. sugar
4 lg. eggs
1 c. milk

2 t. vanilla
2-2/3 c. flour
1-1/2 t. baking powder
1/2 t. salt

Cream butter and sugar together. Add eggs one at a time and beat well after each one. In a separate bowl, combine milk and vanilla. In another bowl sift flour, baking powder, and salt together. Add to batter mixture alternately beginning with milk and ending with flour. Beat well. Pour into loaf pans. Bake at 350 degrees for one hour. Cool on wire racks then invert loaf onto serving plate.

The mother's heart is the child's schoolroom.

-Henry Ward Beecher

Buttermilk Biscuits

Vickie

*Serve these warm from the oven with Tin Can Butter
or homemade jam.*

2 c. flour
1 t. baking soda
1 t. cream of tartar

1/8 t. salt
3 T. shortening
1 c. buttermilk

Cut dry ingredients and shortening together to make fine crumbs. Add buttermilk, stirring with fork until soft dough is formed. Roll 1/2-inch thick and cut with biscuit cutter. Bake at 450 degrees for 10 to 12 minutes or until lightly browned. Makes one dozen biscuits.

Tin Can Butter:

Place heavy cream in a quart or half-gallon can, tighten down the lid and give to your children to roll across the floor! In 15 to 30 minutes you'll have freshly "churned" butter!

The King asked the Queen, and
the Queen asked the
Dairymaid: "Could we have
some butter for the royal
slice of bread?"

-A. A. Milne

Old-fashioned Breads

Cinnamon-Carrot Nut Bread

Pat Habiger
Spearville, KS

*A dark, easy-to-make bread that will stay moist for days...
if it lasts that long!*

2-1/2 c. carrots, shredded
1 c. pecans, finely chopped
2 c. unbleached flour
1-1/2 c. sugar
2 t. baking powder

2 t. cinnamon
1 t. salt
3 eggs
1-1/2 c. vegetable oil
2 t. vanilla

In a medium bowl, toss together the carrots and pecans and set aside. In another bowl, stir together flour, sugar, baking powder, cinnamon and salt. Set aside. In a large mixing bowl, beat eggs with electric mixer. Beat in oil and vanilla. Gradually beat in flour mixture, then carrot mixture. Turn into a well-greased 10" tube pan. Bake at 325 degrees for one hour and 10 minutes or until toothpick inserted in center comes out clean. Cool completely. Makes 24 servings.

For a family picnic, fill a granite-enamel pail with crushed ice and lots of ice cream treats!

Blueberry Bread

Gail Prendergast
Lancaster, PA

This recipe has been handed down in my family for many years.
A great sweet and tart bread.

1 c. sugar
3 c. plus 2 t. flour, divided
1 t. salt
4 t. baking powder
1 egg, beaten

1 c. milk
2 T. butter, melted
juice of half a lemon
1 c. blueberries

Sift together sugar, 3 cups of flour, salt and baking powder in a bowl. Add egg, milk and butter. Do not beat, mix with a wooden spoon. Add lemon juice. Toss blueberries with 2 teaspoons of flour, fold into mixture. Spread in prepared loaf pan and bake at 350 degrees for one hour.

A good laugh is sunshine in the house.

-Thackeray

Old-fashioned Breads

Lemon Clover Rolls

Liz Kenneweg
Gooseberry Patch

This recipe came in a cookbook my mother received from family members when she first got married...it's over 50 years old.

2 c. all-purpose flour
3/4 t. baking soda
1/2 t. salt
1/4 c. plus 2 t. sugar, divided

1/3 c. shortening
1/2 c. milk
3 T. lemon juice

Sift, then measure flour. Sift again with the baking soda, salt and 1/4 cup sugar. Cut shortening into flour mixture until it resembles cornmeal. Combine milk and lemon juice; add to flour mixture. Stir quickly to form a soft dough. Turn onto a lightly floured board. Knead slightly. Form dough into balls about the size of marbles. Place 3 balls in each lightly oiled muffin tin. Sprinkle with remaining sugar. Bake at 450 degrees for 20 minutes. Makes 12 rolls.

Cut out heart shapes from worn-out quilts, stuff them, sew closed and stitch an old button on the front. Pile them in an old tin pan or yelloware mixing bowl!

Muffin Pan Rolls

Kathie Stout
Worthington, OH

Easy to make; so delicious with apple butter!

1 pkg. dry yeast
3/4 c. warm water
2 c. flour, sifted and divided
3/4 t. salt

1-1/2 T. sugar
1 egg
2 T. shortening, melted

Dissolve yeast in warm water, let stand 3 minutes. Add one cup flour, salt, sugar, egg and shortening. Beat until smooth. Add remaining flour and stir until flour is fully blended in. Let rise until double in size, about 30 minutes. Spoon into muffin pans. Let rise again for 30 minutes. Bake at 425 degrees for 15 minutes.

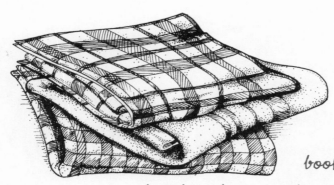

Friends, books, a cheerful heart and a conscience clear are the most choice companions we have here.

-William Mather

Aunt Hazel's French Bread

Dar Stuart
Battle Ground, WA

A recipe I have made for 21 years; it's easy and excellent every time!

2 t. salt
1 pt. boiling water
1/4 c. plus 1 t. honey, divided
2 T. vegetable oil

2 T. yeast
1/2 c. warm water
6 to 8 c. flour

Mix salt, boiling water, 1/4 cup honey and vegetable oil together and let cool in mixing bowl. In a separate bowl add yeast, warm water and remaining honey. Mix and set aside for 10 minutes. Add yeast mixture to water mixture. Add flour until dough is no longer sticky, between 6 to 8 cups. Using a dough hook in a heavy duty mixer, mix the dough for 10 minutes, 5 times. On 6th time turn out on floured board and shape into 2 loaves. Let rise 30 minutes, then slice the top diagonally. Bake at 400 degrees for 20 minutes. Remove bread from oven and brush top with butter while still hot.

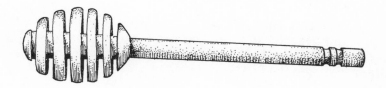

An old-fashioned wooden ladder that's been attached to hooks in your kitchen ceiling, is the perfect place to display your basket collection...tie the baskets on with several strands of raffia.

Cinnamon Streusel Quick Bread

Jana Warnell
Kalispell, MT

*As a newlywed, the best compliments are always from my husband.
He really loves this bread and I love making it for him, so it's never
long before I have to make another loaf!*

2 c. flour
4 t. baking powder
1-1/4 t. salt
1/3 c. oil
2 eggs

1 c. sugar
1-1/2 t. cinnamon
1 c. buttermilk
2 t. vanilla

Heat oven to 350 degrees. Grease and flour bottom only of one
9"x5" pan or 2 8"x4" loaf pans. Combine all ingredients and beat
3 minutes at medium speed. Pour half the batter into the prepared pan.

Streusel:

1/2 c. brown sugar
1 t. cinnamon

2 T. butter, softened

Combine all ingredients and mix well. Sprinkle over batter. Pour the
rest of the batter over the streusel. You can make extra streusel for the
top. Bake at 350 degrees for 45 to 55 minutes in a 9"x5" pan. Remove
from pan immediately and cool on wire racks.

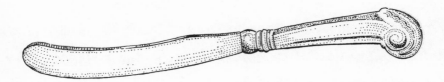

The best antique is an old friend.

- Anonymous

Corn Spoon Bread

Crystal Lappie
Worthington, OH

An old-fashioned favorite. My husband and I enjoy it with a hot bowl of chili or home-style beef stew.

1/2 c. butter
17-oz. can whole kernel corn, drained

16-1/2 oz. can cream-style corn
8-1/2 oz. pkg. corn muffin mix
1 c. sour cream

Preheat oven to 350 degrees. Place butter in a 12"x7" baking pan, place pan in oven until butter melts. Add remaining ingredients to baking pan and mix well. Bake at 350 degrees for 25 to 30 minutes or until golden brown.

Bachelor's fare: bread and cheese and kisses.

–Jonathan Swift

Grandmother's Rolls

Sally Foor
Jeromesville, OH

Make these rolls a family tradition in your home. They're golden and so delicious!

1 c. shortening
3/4 c. sugar
2 t. salt
1 c. boiling water
2 pkgs. dry yeast

1/2 c. lukewarm water
3 lg. eggs
7-1/2 c. sifted flour
1 c. cold water
1 T. oil

Cream shortening, sugar and salt. Add boiling water. Stir until smooth. Dissolve yeast in lukewarm water. Beat eggs, add to yeast mixture. When shortening mixture is lukewarm, add yeast and egg mixture. Add flour alternately with cold water. Stir until dough is smooth. Lightly oil the top and cover tightly with wax paper. Put a piece of aluminum foil over the paper, securing tightly. Place in refrigerator overnight. Remove dough from refrigerator 3 hours before baking. Punch dough down and let rest a 5 minutes. Shape into walnut-sized balls, 3 to a lightly oiled muffin pan. Let formed rolls rest in a warm place until they fill the pans. Bake at 400 degrees for 12 minutes. Makes 48 cloverleaf rolls.

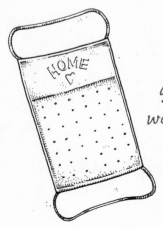

Grandma's old candle box looks wonderful filled with your favorite potpourri and a pillar candle!

Old-fashioned Breads

Country Inn Soda Bread

Abel Darling Bed & Breakfast
Litchfield, CT

Many of our guests have gone home with this recipe; it's always a favorite at the inn.

3 c. flour
1/2 c. raisins
1/2 c. golden raisins
1/2 c. currants
2 t. baking powder

1 t. salt
1/2 c. sugar
1-1/2 c. buttermilk
3 t. caraway seeds

In a large bowl combine all ingredients together mixing thoroughly. Oil a cast-iron skillet, place dough inside and bake at 350 degrees for 45 minutes.

I never had a piece of toast, particularly long and wide, but fell upon the sanded floor, and always on the buttered side.

–James Payne

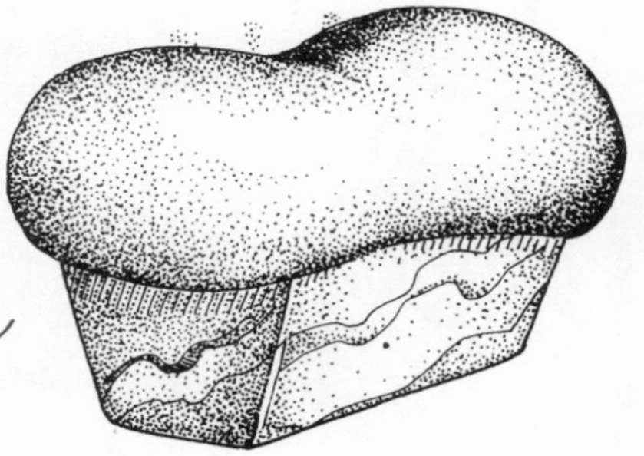

Mile-High Biscuits

Gail Banasiak
Dayton, OH

A golden-brown biscuit, perfect served with honey-butter. For an easy breakfast, make them the night before and refrigerate biscuits on your baking sheet until morning.

2 c. flour
4 t. baking powder
1 T. sugar
1/2 t. salt

1/2 c. shortening
1 egg, beaten
2/3 c. milk

Preheat oven to 450 degrees. Sift together dry ingredients into a large bowl. Cut in shortening with a pastry cutter until mixture resembles coarse crumbs. Combine egg and milk with a whisk, then add all at once to flour mixture. Stir with a fork only until dough follows it around bowl. Turn dough out onto a lightly floured board. Knead very gently with the heels of your hands about 5 to 7 times. Dough will be very moist. Pat or roll out dough to 3/4-inch thickness. Cut in 2-inch squares. Place on an ungreased baking sheet, one inch apart. You can now refrigerate the biscuits until ready to bake, or bake at 450 degrees for 10 to 12 minutes or until golden brown. Makes one dozen.

A cobalt blue pitcher adds beautiful color to your kitchen! Fill it with kitchen utensils or a bright yellow sunflower!

46

Country-Kitchen Potato Bread

Kathie Stout
Worthington, OH

A wonderful old recipe. Perfect every time!

1 lg. potato, peeled and diced	1/2 c. powdered milk
1 c. water	3 eggs
1 t. salt	2 pkgs. active dry yeast
1/2 c. butter	1/4 c. warm water
1/2 c. sugar	6 c. flour

Place the potato, water and salt in a large saucepan. Boil, covered, until potato is tender. Remove from heat, but do not drain. Add butter and sugar and beat with an electric mixer until smooth. Beat in powdered milk and eggs. Dissolve yeast in 1/4 cup warm water and add to mixture. With a wooden spoon, beat in enough flour to make a soft dough, about 4 cups. Work in remaining flour until smooth, turning out onto a floured board if necessary. Place dough in a generously buttered large bowl, turning it over so top is greased.
Cover with a damp towel and set in a warm place. Let rise until doubled, about 1-1/2 hours. Punch down, cover, and refrigerate overnight. The next day, let rise at room temperature for several hours. Divide dough into 2 9"x5" buttered loaf pans. Cover and let rise again until doubled, about one hour. Bake at 375 degrees for 35 to 40 minutes. Set on wire racks to cool.

Babies are such a nice way to start people.

—Don Herold

Sweet Potato Biscuits

Kathy Jo Croom
Bailey, CO

A family favorite in our home and a great take-along snack for traveling.

29-oz. can yams, drained and mashed
1/2 c. butter or margarine, softened
1/2 c. sugar

2 T. milk
1 t. salt
3-1/2 to 4 c. flour
4-1/2 t. baking powder
cinnamon to taste

Combine yams, butter or margarine, sugar, milk and salt. Mix thoroughly. Sift flour, baking powder and cinnamon together. Add to yam mixture. Mix with hands to form a soft dough, adding more flour if needed. On a floured surface, roll dough to one-inch thickness. Cut with cookie cutter and place on greased baking sheet. Bake at 350 degrees for 15 to 20 minutes or until light golden brown. Makes 2 dozen.

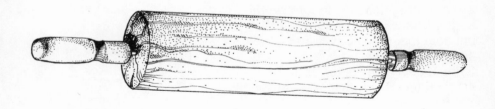

Bread is the warmest, kindest of words. Write it always with a capital letter, like your own name.

–Russian Café Sign

Corn Fritters

Barbara Arnold
Toledo, OH

Wonderful served with fresh butter and maple syrup.

1-1/2 c. flour
14-1/2 oz. can cream-style corn
1 egg

2 T. sugar
1 T. baking powder
vegetable oil

In medium bowl, combine all ingredients, except oil. In a large skillet, pour oil to a depth of 1/2 inch and heat. Drop batter from rounded tablespoons into hot oil. Fry 2 minutes on each side or until golden brown. Remove from skillet and drain on paper towels.

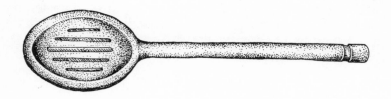

English Muffins

Donna Dye
Ray, OH

I like to add cranberries to the mix!

1 pkg. active dry yeast
1-1/2 c. warm water
3 T. sugar
1/2 c. powdered milk
1 t. salt

1 egg, beaten
3 T. butter
4 c. flour
cornmeal

Dissolve yeast in warm water. Add next 5 ingredients, blend in flour. Let rise until double in bulk. Punch down and shape muffins, flattening slightly. Oil griddle surface and lightly scatter with cornmeal. Cook muffins as you would pancakes, turning when golden.

Garlic Pull-Aparts

Liz Plotnick
Gooseberry Patch

So easy to make! Serve warm with herb butter.

1 loaf frozen whole wheat or
    white bread dough, thawed,
    cut into 32 pieces
1/3 c. butter, melted

2 T. fresh parsley, chopped
2 T. onion, finely chopped
1 t. fresh garlic, finely chopped
1/4 t. salt

Place bread dough in a large mixing bowl. In a smaller bowl, combine remaining ingredients. Pour over bread dough. Toss to coat well. Arrange bread dough in greased 1-1/2 quart casserole or 1-1/2 quart souffle pan. Cover and let rise in warm place until double in size. Heat oven to 375 degrees. Bake for 30 to 35 minutes or until golden brown. If bread begins to brown too quickly, shield with aluminum foil. Cool 10 minutes. Invert pan to remove bread. Serve warm. Serves 8.

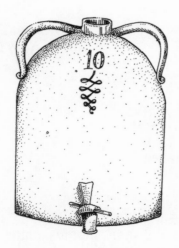

Attach pegs to the long side of an old-fashioned gameboard...a wonderful peg rack to display bundles of your favorite herbs!

Simmering Soups

On a cool autumn day, we'd gather together as a family and drive until we found a farm stand. Corn stalks surrounded the fence posts, Indian corn was swinging from the beams and baskets were overflowing with gourds, apples and pumpkins! Everywhere we looked there were crates of eggs, jugs of freshly-pressed cider, and heaps of potatoes for sale!

The most exciting thing for the kids, however, was picking pumpkins! We'd always need one that was just ours, and Mom needed a few small ones for the porch, windowsills and steps...the ride home was always a little crowded!

After arriving home, we'd find just the right place for each pumpkin while Mom prepared a hearty stew or chowder to warm us up. It always required slow simmering and made the house smell so nice. When it was done, she'd call us inside. We'd peel off jackets and sweaters and sit down to homemade soup served in thick white bowls...perfect on such a clear, crisp day!

Italian Chicken Stew

LaRayne Cummons
Lakeview, OH

My grandsons like this soup after a day of raking leaves or chopping wood. It really warms them up!

1 med. onion, chopped
1 T. oil
28-oz. can whole tomatoes
2 potatoes, peeled and diced
1 t. dried basil
1/2 t. garlic salt

1/2 t. dried oregano
1/4 t. black pepper
10-oz. pkg. frozen mixed
  vegetables
1 c. chicken, cooked and
  chopped

In a 4-quart saucepan, sauté onion in oil until tender. Stir in tomatoes with liquid, potatoes and seasonings. Bring to a boil; reduce heat and simmer, covered, for 10 minutes. Add vegetables and chicken, simmer, covered, for 25 minutes.

Good manners:
The noise you don't make when
you're eating soup.

–Bennett Cerf

Broccoli Cheddar Soup

Donna Nowicki
Center City, MN

*We serve this creamy soup with warm, crusty bread. It's a hearty,
complete meal and so comforting on a crisp evening.*

3/4 c. onion, finely chopped
3/4 c. butter
3/4 c. all-purpose flour
1 t. salt
1 t. black pepper

3 c. chicken broth
4-1/2 c. milk
3 c. fresh broccoli, chopped and
  cooked
3/4 c. Cheddar cheese, shredded

In a saucepan, sauté the onion in butter until tender. Stir in flour, salt
and pepper. Cook and stir until smooth and bubbly. Add broth and milk
all at once. Cook and stir until the mixture boils and thickens. Add
broccoli. Simmer, stirring constantly until heated through. Remove
from heat. Stir in cheese until melted. Serves 6.

*Do not wish for any
other blessing than
a good wife and
rich soup.*

–Russian proverb

Farmstead Split Pea Soup

JoAnn

Fill a thermos with this hearty soup…terrific for an autumn picnic.

8 c. water
1-lb. bag split peas, rinsed and drained
1 ham bone with meat
2 lg. onions, chopped
3 leeks, white part only, chopped
2 celery ribs, chopped
1 lg. carrot, peeled and chopped
1 c. dry white wine
1 clove garlic, finely chopped
1/2 t. dried marjoram
1/4 t. dried thyme
salt and pepper to taste

In Dutch oven, combine all ingredients except salt and pepper. Bring to a boil. Reduce heat, cover and simmer for 2 to 2-1/2 hours or until peas are soft. Remove ham bone and cool to warm. Remove meat from bone and add meat to Dutch oven. Salt and pepper to taste.

A stack of stools is a wonderful way to display children's alphabet blocks, old-fashioned toys, Shaker boxes, candles, or filled apothecary jars.

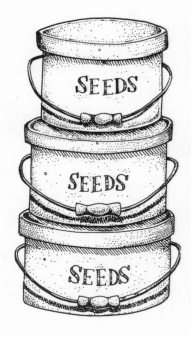

Grandma's Chili

Cheryl Waite
DeKalb, IL

This recipe was passed down from my grandmother to my mother, who passed it on to me. The bacon gives it a special flavor!

4 strips bacon, diced
1-1/2 lbs. ground beef
1 lg. onion, chopped
1/2 c. green pepper, chopped
3 lg. tomatoes, chopped
2 t. sugar

1 t. salt
1 garlic clove
1 T. chili powder
16-oz. can tomato sauce
2 1-lb. cans kidney beans,
   drained

In a medium skillet, fry bacon until crisp. Remove from skillet and drain on paper towels. Add ground beef and cook thoroughly. Add next 8 ingredients and simmer for one hour. Add beans and cook an additional 20 minutes. You can also prepare this chili in your slow cooker; cook on low temperature for 6 to 8 hours.

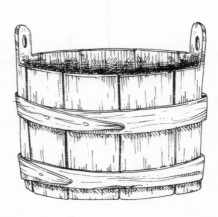

Set children's blocks, old-fashioned school books or a child's lunch bucket on your old schoolhouse chair.

Norwegian Soup Au Gratin

Eleanor Bierley
Miamisburg, OH

A family winter-time tradition! We love to get together to share this warm soup and memories on a cold winter night.

3 T. butter
1/4 lb. hard salami, sliced and
  chopped into 1/2-inch pieces
1/2 c. carrots, thinly sliced
1/3 c. scallions, chopped
1 clove garlic, minced
2-1/2 c. water
1 c. cabbage, shredded

2 T. orzo
2 t. chicken bouillon
1/4 t. pepper
1 T. parsley flakes
1/2 c. heavy cream
8 slices French bread
3/4 c. Swiss or mozzarella
  cheese, shredded

In a large saucepan, melt butter. Sauté salami, carrots, scallions and garlic for 5 minutes. Add water, cabbage, macaroni, chicken bouillon, and pepper. Lower heat. Cover and simmer 12 minutes. Add parsley. Continue to simmer an additional 3 minutes. Stir in heavy cream. Pour equally into 4 10-ounce soup crocks. Top each with 2 slices French bread, side by side. Sprinkle equally with shredded cheese. Broil 3 to 5 minutes until cheese melts and becomes golden.

Happiness often sneaks in through a door you didn't know you left open.

—John Barrymore

Tomato Bisque

Sandy Spayer
Jeromesville, OH

An old-fashioned favorite! Perfect with a grilled cheese sandwich!

2 c. chicken broth or stock
14-1/2 oz. can whole tomatoes,
   undrained and broken up
1/2 c. celery, chopped
1/2 c. onion, chopped

3 med. tomatoes, peeled, seeded
   and chopped
3 T. butter
3 T. flour
2 c. half-and-half
1 T. sugar

In large saucepan, combine broth, canned tomatoes, celery, and onion; bring to a boil. Reduce heat. Cover and simmer 20 minutes. In blender or food processor, purée mixture in small batches until all mixture is puréed. In same pan, cook fresh tomatoes in butter about 5 minutes. Stir in flour. Add half-and-half. Over low heat, cook and stir until thickened. Stir in broth mixture and sugar. Heat through, do not boil.

Old wooden storage boxes look great with the drawers slightly open. Fill them with dried orange slices, pepperberries, herbs or potpourri.

Simmering Soups

Onion Soup

Mary Murray
Gooseberry Patch

One of our favorites! Try Vidalia onions for a sweeter taste.

2 T. butter
5 med. yellow onions, thinly
  sliced
2 T. sugar
3-1/2 c. beef broth
5 c. water

1/2 t. salt
1/2 t. black pepper
4 slices French bread
4 T. Gruyère cheese, grated

In a 5-quart Dutch oven, melt butter over medium-high heat. Add onions and sugar and sauté until onions are lightly golden, about 10 minutes. Reduce the heat to low and sauté 10 more minutes, stirring often. Add broth and water, bring to a boil over high heat. Reduce heat to simmer and cook uncovered for 20 minutes. Salt and pepper to taste, bring just to boiling over high heat. Ladle soup into 4 8-ounce oven proof soup bowls, place bowls on a baking sheet. Top each bowl with a slice of toasted French bread and sprinkle with one tablespoon cheese. Bake uncovered at 400 degrees until grated cheese is melted, about 5 minutes. Serves 4.

It is probably illegal to make soups, stews and casseroles without plenty of onions.

-Maggie Waldron

Barley Vegetable Soup

Karen Urfer
New Philadelphia, OH

A great soup our family enjoys after raking leaves or a winter snowball fight!

1/2 lb. ground turkey
1/2 c. onion, chopped
1 clove garlic, pressed
7 c. water
1-lb. 12 oz. can stewed tomatoes
1/2 c. med. size barley
1/2 c. celery, sliced
1/2 c. carrots, sliced

2 beef bouillon cubes
1/2 t. dried basil
1 bay leaf
salt and pepper to taste
9-oz. pkg. frozen mixed
    vegetables

In a Dutch oven, brown the turkey. Add the onion and garlic. Cook until tender. Stir in all remaining ingredients except the frozen vegetables. Cover and bring to a boil. Reduce heat and simmer for one hour. Add the frozen vegetables and cook an additional 15 minutes. Add additional water if needed.

Only the pure in heart can make good soup.

—Beethoven

Simmering Soups

Broccoli Cheese Noodle Soup *Debbie Cummons-Parker*
Lakeview, OH

A creamy soup that's really filling.

3/4 c. onion, chopped
2 T. oil
6 c. boiling water
6 chicken-flavored
    bouillon cubes
8-oz. pkg. noodles
20-oz. pkg. frozen broccoli,
    chopped

1 lb. processed cheese
6 c. milk
1 t. salt
dash of pepper
dash of garlic powder

Sauté onion in oil. Set aside. To the boiling water, add bouillon cubes, noodles and broccoli. Cook until tender. Add onion, cheese, milk, salt, pepper and garlic powder. Cover and let simmer. Soup can be made ahead and frozen. To reheat, either use a double boiler or microwave, as it scorches easily. Serves 16.

Laughter is the brush that sweeps away the cobwebs of the heart.

– Mort Walker

Chicken Mulligan

Judy Kelly
St. Charles, MO

I first served this at a casual New Year's Eve party…it can be made ahead of time and simply reheated before guests arrive.

2 or 3 whole chickens, skinned, cut up
4 16-oz. cans pork and beans
16-oz. can tomatoes, chopped
16-oz. can corn, drained
2 16-oz cans lima beans
1 lb. cabbage, shredded
1 lb. carrots, sliced

1 bunch celery, chopped
46-oz. can vegetable juice cocktail
14-oz. bottle catsup
1 lg. onion, chopped
2 lbs. potatoes, diced
salt and pepper to taste

Rinse the chicken and pat dry. Bake, covered at 375 degrees for one hour. Reserve the drippings in a bowl. Cool. Skim the surface. Remove the meat from the bone. Cut into one-inch pieces. Combine the and chicken in a 3-gallon stockpot. Add the pork and beans, tomatoes, corn, lima beans, cabbage, carrots, celery, vegetable juice, catsup, onion, potatoes, salt and pepper. Simmer for 1-1/2 hours, stirring frequently. Serves 20.

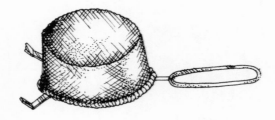

A new baby is like the beginning of all things…wonder, hope, a dream of possibilities.

–Eda J. Le Shan

Simmering Soups

Old-Fashioned Beef Stew

Linda Romano
Canonsburg, PA

I love to dip Italian bread in this soup!

2 T. oil
3 cloves garlic, minced
1-1/2 lbs. beef stew meat
2 c. water
1/2 c. tomato sauce or juice
1 bay leaf

salt and pepper
3 potatoes, cubed
2 carrots, diced
2 c. frozen green beans
2 T. French onion soup mix
flour

In Dutch oven, sauté oil, garlic and stew meat until brown. Add the water, tomato sauce or juice and bay leaf. Salt and pepper to taste. Cover and let simmer for an hour. After one hour add the potatoes, carrots, and green beans. Sprinkle with French onion soup mix. Cook for 30 minutes or until all is tender. Add flour as needed to thicken. Serves 4 to 6.

Don't be afraid to take big steps. You can't cross a chasm in two small jumps.

−David L. George

Cheesy Potato Soup

Kim Roepke
Omaha, NE

A big bowl of this creamy soup is perfect comfort food.

1/2 c. carrots, chopped	1/2 t. salt
1/4 c. onion, chopped	1/8 t. pepper
1/2 c. celery, chopped	1 chicken bouillon cube
3 c. potatoes, diced	2 T. flour
1 t. parsley	1-1/2 c. milk
1 c. water	1/2 lb. processed cheese

Combine first 9 ingredients and simmer until vegetables are done. Blend together flour and milk in a separate bowl. Add to the vegetables, stirring constantly, until soup thickens. When soup is thickened, add processed cheese. Stir until all is melted.

Hand-paint or stencil stars, hearts, or a flag design on a plain peg rack; then hang on an old-fashioned straw hat!

Simmering Soups

Turkey-Vegetable Chowder

Robyn Fiedler
Tacoma, WA

This is a terrific hearty chowder!

1/4 c. butter
2 med. onions, chopped
2 T. flour
1 t. curry powder
3 c. chicken broth
1 lg. russet potato, chopped
1 c. carrots, thinly sliced

1 c. celery, thinly sliced
2 T. fresh parsley
1/2 t. dried sage or poultry
  seasoning
3 c. cooked turkey, cubed
1-1/2 c. half-and-half
10-oz. pkg. frozen spinach

Melt butter in pan. Add onions and sauté for 10 minutes. Stir in flour and curry powder. Cook for 2 minutes. Add broth, potatoes, carrots, celery, parsley and sage. Reduce heat to low. Cover and simmer 10 to 15 minutes. Add turkey, half-and-half and frozen spinach. Cover and simmer, stirring occasionally until heated through, about 10 minutes.

If people concentrated on the really important things in life, there'd be a shortage of fishing poles.

-Doug Larson

Slow-Cooker Chicken Stew

Mary Ann Nemecek
Springfield, IL

A very comforting soup any time of year...wonderful with freshly-baked bread.

2 onions, chopped
2 chicken breasts, cubed and
    sprinkled with Greek
    seasoning
1 lb. baby carrots
6 med. potatoes, cubed with
    skins

4-oz. can sliced mushrooms,
    undrained
2 10-3/4 oz. cans cream of
    mushroom soup

Combine all ingredients. Cook on high for 2 hours and then on low for 5 to 6 hours.

Friendship is a word the very sight of which in print makes the heart warm.

-Augustine Birrell

Simmering Soups

Senate Bean Soup

Linda Littlejohn
Greensboro, NC

A homemade soup that's wonderful for chilly days or nights!

1lb. white beans
cold water
1 ham bone
1 c. mashed potatoes

2 onions, chopped
2 c. celery, chopped
2 garlic cloves, minced
1/4 c. parsley, chopped

Soak beans overnight in 2-1/2 cups cold water. Drain and put in kettle with ham bone and 3 quarts of water. Bring to boil and simmer for 2 hours. Stir in potatoes, onions, celery, garlic and parsley. Simmer for approximately one hour or until beans are cooked. Remove meat from bones and return to soup.

Wisdom is the reward you get for a lifetime of listening when you'd have preferred to talk.

—Doug Larson

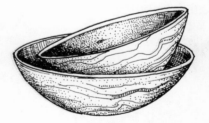

Traditional Wedding Soup

Marisa Adams
Manchester, CT

Every summer our family would travel to Pennsylvania with my cousins. The kids, nine in all, would create fun games to pass the time! Now, years later, we still try to get together, even if only for a few days.

4 lg. ripe tomatoes, peeled,
   seeded and chopped
2 qts. chicken broth
1 head escarole, washed and
   chopped

1 T. dried basil
1 T. dried parsley
black pepper
Garnish: fresh parsley,
   Parmesan cheese

Reserve juice from tomatoes. Heat broth and when it comes to a boil, add remaining ingredients, except meatballs. Bring to a boil and add meatballs a few at a time. Bring to a boil again, reduce heat and simmer until meatballs are thoroughly cooked, about one hour. Serve with fresh parsley and Parmesan cheese sprinkled on top.

Meatballs:

1 lb. hamburger
1 egg
1 clove garlic, minced

1 T. dried parsley
1/4 c. bread crumbs
1/4 c. Parmesan cheese

Combine all ingredients together until thoroughly combined. Roll into golf ball-size portions. Set aside until ready to add to soup mixture.

Homestyle Broccoli Soup

Pat Habiger
Spearville, KS

This really warms you up on a chilly autumn day!

1 bunch broccoli, chopped
2 c. water
1 stick margarine
1 med. onion, chopped
2 celery stalks, chopped
2 carrots, peeled and chopped
1/2 to 3/4 c. flour

2 potatoes, peeled and chopped
2 c. milk
3 c. hot chicken broth
1 t. celery salt
1 t. garlic powder
1 T. parsley, chopped
salt and pepper to taste

Steam broccoli over water until tender; reserve water. In large soup pot, melt margarine, add onion, celery and carrots. Sauté for 3 to 5 minutes. Add flour, stirring quickly. Cook about 2 minutes over medium heat. Slowly add liquid from broccoli, stirring constantly. Add broccoli and remaining ingredients. Mix well. Cook over very low heat for 1-1/2 to 2 hours stirring often to prevent scorching. Can be made in a slow cooker.

We all have our "good old days" tucked away inside our hearts, and we return to them in dreams like cats to favorite armchairs.

—Brian Carter

ili

Dorothy Jackson
Weddington, NC

Every Thanksgiving for the last 17 years, our family has gathered together either at the ocean, mountains or at home to spend time together. Fireside Chili is usually cooking while the adults are catching up on events within the family and the children are running around! No matter when or where this chili is served, it will always remind me of these special family times together.

1-1/2 lbs. ground beef or pork
1 c. green pepper, chopped
1 c. onion, chopped
2 15-oz. cans red kidney beans, drained
28-oz. can tomatoes, chopped and undrained
15-oz. can tomato sauce
1-1/2 c. water

2 T. chili powder
2 T. Worcestershire sauce
1 T. honey
1 t. salt
1/2 t. dried basil
1/2 t. cinnamon
1/4 t. allspice, ground
1 lg. bay leaf

In a 4-quart Dutch oven, cook meat with green peppers and onions until meat is browned and vegetables are tender. Drain fat. Add kidney beans, undrained tomatoes, tomato sauce, water, chili powder, Worcestershire sauce, honey, salt, basil, cinnamon, allspice and bay leaf. Simmer uncovered for 30 minutes. Cover and simmer for one hour stirring occasionally. Serves 6 to 8.

Heaven is a pot of chili
simmering on the stove.

—Charles Simic

Hearty Minestrone

Teresa Sullivan
Westerville, OH

This soup is worth the extra time it takes to prepare...you may even want to double the recipe!

2 slices bacon, diced
1/4 lb. ham, diced
1/2 lb. Italian sausage, diced
1 lg. onion, chopped
3 cloves garlic, chopped
3 stalks celery, chopped
1 lg. leek, chopped
2 sm. zucchini, chopped
2 qt. beef stock

1/2 c. dried kidney beans, soaked overnight in cold water
1/2 head cabbage, shredded
1 c. dry red wine
16-oz. can tomatoes, cut up
1/2 c. elbow macaroni
pepper to taste
2 t. dried basil
Parmesan cheese, grated

Cook bacon, ham and sausage in a large skillet. Add onions, garlic, celery, leek, and zucchini. Cook 10 minutes. Heat stock in a large kettle. Add contents of skillet, drained kidney beans, cabbage and wine. Simmer, partially covered for 90 minutes. Add tomatoes, macaroni, pepper and basil. Cook 15 minutes. Serve with cheese.

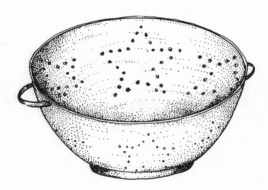

Where we love is home...home that our feet may leave, but not our hearts.

–Oliver Wendell Homes, Sr.

:getable Beef Soup

Alicia Bates
Kent, OH

I can remember coming home after school and smelling the aroma of this soup and homemade bread. Even today it still takes me back!

1 lb. ground beef
3 c. water
1 c. carrots, sliced
1 c. celery, chopped
1 c. onion, chopped
2 c. potatoes, diced

1 t. salt
1 t. browning sauce
1/4 t. pepper
1 t. basil
1 bay leaf
28-oz. can tomatoes

Sauté ground beef, breaking up with spoon until well browned. Drain well. Stir in remaining ingredients. Heat to boiling, reduce heat. Cover and simmer 20 minutes or until veggies are tender. Remove bay leaf before serving.

One of the oldest human needs is having someone to wonder where you are when you don't come home at night.

-Margaret Mead

Camp Stew

Peg Ackerman
Pasadena, CA

On a cool, fall evening, I always make this recipe. It's wonderful for a family campout or informal dinner with friends.

1-1/2 to 2 lbs. fresh carrots	1 c. biscuit mix
6 to 7 russet potatoes	salt and pepper
2 med. onions	butter
4 lbs. stew beef	2 envelopes stew seasoning

Preheat oven to 350 degrees. Wash carrots, remove tops and tips but do not peel. Cut into thirds. Wash potatoes. Do not peel. Cut in half. Larger ones should be quartered. Remove skin from onions and cut into quarters. Cut up meat into 2-inch pieces. Put biscuit mix in a large plastic bag and sprinkle salt and pepper. Put one tablespoon butter in a large skillet to melt. Put a portion of the meat in the biscuit mix and shake to coat meat. Put meat in skillet and brown on all sides. When the meat is browned, put it in a large stew pot or roasting pan. Continue with the rest of the meat. Add carrots, potatoes, onions, to pan and mix. Put in seasoning, sprinkling on stew. Add water to cover everything and mix with large spoon. Cover and cook at 350 degrees for 1-1/2 to 2 hours in oven or 2 to 2-1/2 hours on camp stove. Stir in 30 minute intervals. Stew is done when potatoes can be cut easily with fork or spoon.

Stencil the alphabet on the outside of an old wooden wagon, then tuck in your children's Teddy bears or dolls!

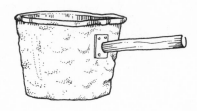

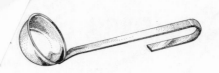

Wild Rice Soup

Maureen Noterman
Adams, MN

We love this thick, rice soup. It really takes the chill out on the cool evenings we get here in Minnesota!

1/2 c. wild rice
2 c. cold water
1/4 c. butter
2/3 c. onions, chopped
2/3 c. celery, chopped

2/3 c. carrots, chopped
4 c. chicken broth
3 T. cornstarch
2-1/4 c. milk, divided
salt and pepper

Soak rice in water for one to 2 hours. Melt butter in saucepan. Add vegetables and sauté for 3 minutes. Add rice and sauté for 5 minutes, stirring occasionally. Add chicken broth. Cover and bring to a boil. Reduce heat. Simmer one hour, rice and vegetables should be tender. Slowly add 2 cups of milk to hot soup, mix well. Dissolve cornstarch in 1/4 cup of cold milk. Use a whisk and add to the soup to thicken. Boil and then let simmer. Add salt and pepper to taste.

Layer potpourri ingredients in one of Grandma's old, wavy glass jars! Tie a square of homespun on the top with raffia and add a rusty tin star or heart...beautiful!

Simmering Soups

Aunt Sandy's Special Chowder

Wendy Lee Paffenroth
Pine Island, NY

This makes the house smell so good! We love to serve it with homemade muffins or crusty Italian bread!

5 slices bacon, diced
5 c. water
1 c. celery, diced
28-oz. can stewed tomatoes
3 potatoes, peeled and sliced
4 carrots, diced
3 onions, diced

2 T. fresh parsley, chopped
1 t. salt
1 t. dried thyme
1/2 t. pepper
1 bay leaf
2 10-oz. cans clams, minced or
    whole, undrained

In a heavy Dutch oven, fry the bacon until almost crisp. Add the water and all remaining ingredients except clams. Heat until boiling and reduce the heat to a low simmer. Cover and cook until the vegetables are tender. Add the clams and juice, cook about another 20 to 30 minutes.

Of soup and love, the first is best.

—Spanish Proverb

...sage Chowder

Kim McGeorge
Ashley, OH

Fresh corn makes this soup so wonderful!

2 c. fresh corn kernels
1 lb. pork sausage
1 c. onions, chopped
4 c. potatoes, diced
2 t. salt
1/2 t. dried marjoram

2 c. water
1/8 t. black pepper
16-oz. can cream-style corn
12-oz. can evaporated milk
Garnish: fresh parsley, chopped

Cook corn in boiling water 4 to 5 minutes; set aside to cool. Brown sausage over medium heat for 5 minutes, add onions; continue cooking 3 more minutes. Add potatoes, salt, marjoram, water and pepper. Bring to a boil, reduce heat to simmer and cook until potatoes are tender. Add both fresh and cream-style corn and evaporated milk. Heat to almost boiling. Ladle chowder into bowls, garnish with parsley.

Create the feel of an old General Store by filling a
wooden bowl with dried apple and orange slices,
cinnamon sticks, rosehips, cloves and star anise;
tuck in a wooden or antique scoop.

P·A·T·C·H·W·O·R·K
Salads

...elight; baskets filled with sun-ripened tom... crisp lettuce, crunchy carrots and red radishes! I can picture Mom's kitchen table, covered with a blue and white checked cloth. Pink and white cosmos in a green enamel pitcher, tall glasses filled to the brim with ice, and a pitcher of tea complete the memory.

Certain country things seem just right in summertime...a salad of just-picked vegetables and an icy glass of tea. These wonderful vegetables never taste the same in winter as they do in summer; fresh from the garden.

Our family always sat on the porch after lunch. Locusts filled the afternoon with their song, a sure sign that summer was moving toward fall. Before evening came, the kids would wade barefoot through the creek, splash one another and enjoy the cool water in the late summer heat.

Summertime Spaghetti Salad

Mary Haubiel
Delaware, OH

We always enjoy this salad at family gatherings or barbecues...it's become a family tradition!

1 lb. flat spaghetti
1-oz. jar dry salad seasoning,
    optional
16-oz. bottle Italian dressing

1 green pepper, chopped
2 green onion bunches, diced
4-oz. jar mushrooms, sliced
1/4 to 1/2 lb. ham, diced

Cook spaghetti in a large pot. Combine remaining ingredients well and toss with cooled spagehetti. Refrigerate overnight, or at least 12 hours.

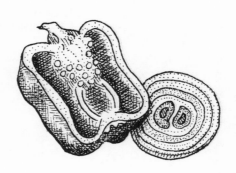

Slip small, old-fashioned iron hooks over a twig or narrow length of barn siding...a wonderful primitive herb rack!

...to Salad

Kathy Williamson
Delaware, OH

I like tru... ilad because I always have the ingredients on hand and it's so simple to make.

1 lb. cherry tomatoes
2 T. chives, chopped
1 T. mint, finely chopped

1 t. sugar
salt and pepper to taste
2 T. white wine vinegar

Slice tomatoes onto a pretty serving dish. Sprinkle with remaining ingredients. Serves 4.

Homemade Blue Cheese Dressing

Pat Akers
Stanton, CA

Salads will never be the same after you taste this fresh dressing!

1 qt. mayonnaise
1 T. onion powder
1 T. seasoned salt

1 T. coarse black pepper
1/2 qt. buttermilk
3 to 4 oz. blue cheese, crumbled

Place mayonnaise in a large mixing bowl, slowly blend in buttermilk. Add dry ingredients one at a time, add cheese. Keeps in the refrigerator for 10 days.

The cherry tomato is a wonderful invention, producing, as it does, a satisfactorily explosive squish when bitten.

—Miss Manners

Carrot & Raisin Salad

Jackie Crough
Salina, KS

Grandma made this salad often. It's always very good!

2 c. carrots, shredded
1 c. raisins

1/2 c. walnuts, chopped
1/2 c. mayonnaise

Mix all ingredients together in a large bowl. Cover and refrigerate overnight. Serve on a bed of lettuce.

Vermicelli Salad

Judy Kelly
St. Charles, MO

Quick and so easy!

1 lb. vermicelli
4 T. oil
1 t. lemon juice
4-oz. jar pimentos, chopped

1 sm. onion, chopped
1 green pepper, chopped
1 pt. mayonnaise
salt, pepper, garlic salt to taste

Cook pasta according to package directions. Rinse and drain. Marinate overnight in oil and lemon juice. The next day, add remaining ingredients, chill and serve.

Paint an old wicker basket mustard yellow, line it with a square of blue homespun and share the extra bounty from your garden with a friend.

Fruit Trifle Salad

Mary Tolle
Upland, CA

*This is always my favorite to serve in summer when strawberries
are fresh and plentiful.*

6 oranges, peeled and sliced
3 bananas, sliced
3 c. blueberries
2 c. seedless grapes
3 c. strawberries, halved

4-oz. pkg. instant vanilla
    pudding
1-3/4 c. milk
3/4 c. dairy sour cream
1 t. orange zest

In a large glass bowl, layer all of the fruit in order listed above. Fruit
can be substituted for in-season items, except melon. For the topping,
combine pudding mix and milk. Beat for one to 2 minutes. Beat in sour
cream and orange peel. Serve with fruit.

*Where is home? Home is where
the heart can laugh
without shyness.
Home is where the
heart's tears can dry at
their own pace.*

-Vernon G. Baker

Vegetable Pasta Salad

Susan Kennedy
Delaware, OH

So easy to make and even better when you use fresh, crunchy vegetables from your garden!

1/4 c. fresh parsley sprigs,
    loosely packed
2 T. salad oil
2 T. wine vinegar
2 T. water
1 or 2 garlic cloves
1/2 t. dry mustard
1/4 t. salt

1/4 t. black pepper
2 oz. linguine noodles, broken
1 carrot, cut into juliene strips
1 turnip, cut into juliene strips
1 zucchini, cut into juliene strips
1/2 c. frozen or fresh peas
2-oz. pkg. mozzarella cheese,
    shredded

To prepare dressing, combine parsley, salad oil, wine vinegar, water, garlic, mustard, salt, and pepper in a blender. Blend until combined. Set aside. Cook linguine according to package directions. Drain and rinse with cold water and drain again. In large salad bowl, combine pasta, carrot, turnip, zucchini, peas and cheese. Add dressing, toss to coat.

Homemade preserves are beautiful displayed in an old-fashioned corner cupboard! Bright red tomatoes, green pickles and golden corn are particularly nice!

Sunflower Salad

Shirley Moteberg
Grandin, ND

This recipe makes a large bowl...just perfect for a family reunion!

8 oz. cream cheese
3-oz. pkg. instant vanilla pudding
3-oz. pkg. instant lemon pudding
15-oz. can crushed pineapple,
    with juice

12-oz. container frozen whipped
    topping
1-1/2 c. sunflower seeds,
    roasted and salted

Soften cream cheese and mix in dry pudding mixes. Stir in pineapple and juice. Fold in frozen whipped topping and sunflower seeds. Refrigerate before serving.

I value the friend who for me finds time on his calendar, but I cherish the friend who for me does not consult his calendar.

—Robert Brault

Banana Salad

Phyllis Laughrey
Mount Vernon, OH

Refreshing and cool, a great warm-weather fruit salad.

2 3-oz. pkgs. lemon gelatin
2 c. boiling water
2 c. cold water or lemon-lime
  soda

1 c. mini marshmallows
2 lg. bananas, diced
2-lb. can crushed pineapple,
  drained

Dissolve gelatin in boiling water. Add cold water or lemon-lime soda. Add marshmallows and allow them to melt. Let set until thick or completely cooled. Place bananas and pineapple in gelatin mixture. Let it set completely.

Custard:

1 c. pineapple juice
1/2 c. sugar
1 T. flour

1/8 t. salt
1 egg
1 c. frozen whipped topping

Cook pineapple juice, sugar, flour, salt and egg until thick. Set aside to cool. Fold whipped topping into cooked custard and spread on top of set gelatin.

Few things are more delightful than grandchildren fighting over your lap.
—Doug Larson

Susie Salad

Sue Lovely
Three Rivers, MI

A recipe handed down to me from my mom; now it's "expected" at most meals!

1 head lettuce, torn
1 sm. onion, chopped
8-oz. pkg. Swiss cheese,
   shredded

10-oz. box frozen peas
salt and pepper to taste
Parmesan cheese

Layer above ingredients in salad bowl. Cover with dressing. Don't mix until ready to serve. Best if refrigerated overnight before serving. Sprinkle Parmesan cheese over dressing if desired.

Dressing:

1/2 c. salad dressing
2 T. sour cream

1/8 c. sugar

Combine all ingredients and pour over salad.

Fill an old sap bucket with blooms from your garden, attach a loop of ribbon and hang it from your doorknob...a lovely way to welcome visitors!

Twelve-Layer Salad

Kristi Warzocha
Lakewood, OH

Layer this salad in a glass bowl so the variety of colors can be seen!

12 oz. peas
1 head iceberg lettuce, shredded
3/4 c. parsley, chopped
4 eggs, hard boiled and chopped
1 red bell pepper, thinly sliced
4 carrots, shredded
1 c. black olives, sliced

2 T. fresh dill, chopped
1 c. radishes, sliced
12 oz. Swiss or Cheddar cheese,
   shredded
1/2 lb. bacon, crisply cooked and
   crumbled
1 red onion, thinly sliced

Cook peas in water until crisp-tender, set aside. Line the bottom of a 3-quart, straight-sided bowl with lettuce. Layer the remaining ingredients in the order listed; adding peas after black olives.

Dressing:

2 c. mayonnaise
1/2 c. sour cream
1/4 c. chives, chopped
2 T. sugar

1 T. tarragon vinegar
salt and pepper to taste
1/2 c. plus 2 T. parsley, chopped

Combine all dressing ingredients and 1/2 cup parsley. Spread half of the dressing over the salad, set aside the remaining dressing to serve on the side. Sprinkle salad with remaining 2 tablespoons parsley. Cover bowl tightly with plastic wrap and refrigerate for 6 to 12 hours.

A child on a farm sees a plane fly overhead and dreams of a faraway place. A traveler on the plane sees the farm house...and dreams of home.

-Carl Burns

Mom's Potato Salad

Jane Goetz
Hays, KS

This recipe reminds me of family get-togethers and camping trips.
Every time I make it, I remember Mom and how special she
was and is to me.

5 lbs. red potatoes
1 doz. eggs
3 T. sugar
3 T. mustard
3 T. horseradish sauce

5 T. dill pickle juice
yellow food coloring, if desired
32-oz. jar mayonnaise
1 sm. onion, chopped

Parboil potatoes with skins on. Hardboil the eggs. Cool both. Peel off the skins and dice the potatoes into a big bowl, shell the eggs and dice into the bowl. In a separate container, mix all the sauce ingredients together. Pour over the potatoes and eggs and mix well. Refrigerate a few hours before serving.

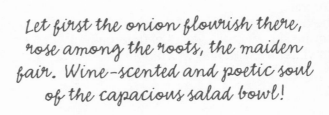

Let first the onion flourish there,
rose among the roots, the maiden
fair. Wine-scented and poetic soul
of the capacious salad bowl!

—Robert Louis Stevenson

Patchwork Salads

Red Potato Salad

Katie Sullivan
Westerville, OH

A traditional red-skin potato salad we like to serve with grilled dishes.

12 med. red potatoes, diced
2 T. French or Russian dressing
1-1/2 c. celery, chopped
8 to 10 green onions, chopped
1/2 red onion, chopped
1/4 green bell pepper, finely chopped
1/4 red bell pepper, finely chopped

1/4 c. sweet pickles, finely chopped
1/4 c. parsley, finely chopped
3 T. chives, finely chopped
7 eggs, hard-cooked
2 t. salt
fresh ground pepper to taste
2/3 c. mayonnaise
Garnish: paprika and parsley

Boil potatoes in water until just tender. Drain and rinse briefly in cold water to stop cooking process. Toss in French or Russian dressing and chill at least 30 minutes. Combine celery, onions, peppers, pickles, parsley and chives with the marinated potatoes. Chop 5 of the eggs, reserving the other 2 for garnish. Add to salad, along with salt, pepper and mayonnaise. Check seasoning. Refrigerate at least 3 hours or overnight. Check seasoning again. Place in serving bowl. Slice remaining 2 eggs and decorate top, sprinkling with paprika and chopped parsley.

Traveling in the company of those we love is home in motion.

-Leigh Hunt

Cranberry Salad

Diane Dodd
Cape Girardeau, MO

I remember this salad so well because my brother and I were very young when it became a tradition to have cranberry salad every Thanksgiving and Christmas. Now, for the past 20 years, I've been bringing it to our family gatherings.

16-oz. pkg. cranberries, frozen
1-1/2 c. sugar
1/2 pt. whipping cream
1 c. mini marshmallows

1-1/2 c. apples, diced
1 c. white grapes, halved
1 c. nuts, chopped

Rinse frozen cranberries under cold running water to wash off any loose stems. Grind or chop frozen cranberries using a food processor or blender. Put chopped cranberries in a large bowl and add sugar. Thoroughly mix by hand and refrigerate overnight. Before serving, whip the 1/2 pint of whipping cream in a separate bowl until peaks form. Fold whipped cream into the cranberry-sugar mixture. Add the marshmallows, apples, grapes and nuts. Mix together and serve.

Family faces are magic mirrors. Looking at people who belong to us, we see the past, present and future. We make discoveries about ourselves.

-Gail Lumet Buckley

Patchwork Salads

Sugar Snap Pea & Bean Salad

Liz Kenneweg
Gooseberry Patch

Freshly-picked beans and peas from your garden make this salad perfect for a warm weather cookout with family and friends!

Dressing:

1 clove garlic, minced
1/4 t. salt
2 T. red wine vinegar
2 t. Dijon mustard

1/8 t. sugar
1/4 c. olive oil
black pepper to taste

Place garlic in a small bowl along with salt, vinegar, mustard and sugar. Mix well then slowly add the olive oil, whisking constantly. Season with pepper and set aside.

Salad:

1/2 lb. green beans
1/2 lb. wax beans
1/4 lb. sugar snap peas
1 lg. shallot, sliced lengthwise
 and cut into thin strips

3 lg. ripe tomatoes, cut into
 one-inch cubes
3/4 c. fresh basil leaves
salt and pepper to taste

Add green beans to a stockpot, cover with water. Bring to a boil and cook until just tender, 3 to 5 minutes. Remove beans with a slotted spoon, drain well; rinse under cold water and drain again. Repeat cooking instructions for both the wax beans and peas. When beans and peas are cooked, pat dry and place in a large bowl. Add shallot and tomatoes. Chop basil by layering the leaves then rolling them together. Slice very thinly and add to the salad. Sprinkle with salt and pepper and toss well. When ready to serve, toss with the vinaigrette. Serves 4 to 6.

Orange-Cranberry Salad

Beth Warner
Delaware, OH

My grandma always made this during the holidays. It has such a refreshing sweet-tart taste!

6 c. raw cranberries
1 orange, sliced
2 c. sugar
1 c. celery, coarsely chopped

1 c. English walnuts, chopped
2 3-oz. pkgs. lemon gelatin
3-1/2 c. hot water

Grind cranberries and orange together. Stir in sugar and allow mixture to stand overnight. The next morning, add celery and nuts. Set aside. Dissolve gelatin in hot water. Set it aside to cool. Stir into cranberry mixture. Chill until firm.

A great flea-market find! A weathered door shutter gives a primitive feel when hung over a window, or attach two shutters together for a wonderful room divider!

Cookie Salad

Crystal Moeller
Hebo, OR

Whenever I make this recipe it reminds me of a dear friend, who first shared it with our family.

2 3-oz. boxes vanilla instant
   pudding
1 c. buttermilk
8 oz. frozen whipped topping
15-oz. can fruit cocktail
2 15-oz. cans mandarin
   oranges

20-oz. can pineapple tidbits
1 pkg. fudge stripe cookies,
   crushed

Mix pudding and buttermilk. Fold in frozen whipped topping. Drain all of the fruit. Separate maraschino cherries from the fruit cocktail and set aside. Add fruit to pudding mixture and mix well. Blend in cookies, reserving 1/2 cup. Sprinkle top of salad with remaining crushed cookies and top with reserved maraschino cherries. Serves 8 to 10.

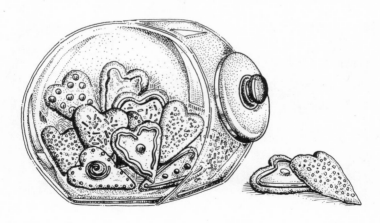

An old candle pan full of colorful, fresh fruit makes a terrific warm-weather centerpiece.

Shimmering Three-Berry Salad

Jo Ann

Berry picking is a fun family outing! Gather everyone together and spend the afternoon picking your favorite berries for this fresh berry-filled salad!

2 c. cranberry juice
2 3-oz. pkgs. gelatin, any red
    flavor

1-1/2 c. club soda
1 t. lemon juice
3 c. assorted berries, divided

Bring cranberry juice to a boil, stir in gelatin until completely dissolved. Stir in club soda and lemon juice. Refrigerate about 1-1/2 hours or until thickened. Stir in 2 cups of the berries. Spoon into 5-cup mold. Refrigerate 4 hours or until firm. Unmold. Top with remaining one cup of berries. Serves 8.

Silences make the real conversations between friends. Not the saying but the never needing to say is what counts.

-Margaret Lee Runbeck

Ribbon Salad

Doris Stegner
Gooseberry Patch

This pretty salad is well worth the time it takes to prepare it...it's very attractive sliced!

6 c. water
6 3-oz. boxes gelatin, different
   flavors and colors

16-oz. carton sour cream

Bring water to a boil. Dissolve one box of gelatin in one cup boiling water. Reserve 1/3 cup gelatin mixture and pour remaining in an 8" square dish. When gelatin is set, mix the reserved 1/3 cup of gelatin with 1/3 cup of sour cream and spread over set gelatin. When the sour cream layer has set, repeat layering with the remaining ingredients until salad has 12 layers.

On days when warmth is the most important need of the human heart, the kitchen is the place you can find it.

-E. B. White

Marinated Vegetables

The Governor's Inn
Ludlow, VT

It's easy to make your own dressing, and it tastes so fresh!

1/2 lb. cheese tortellini, cooked
    and drained
1 c. broccoli flowerets
1 c. cauliflower flowerets
20-oz. can pineapple chunks,
    drained

6-oz. can pitted black olives,
    drained
1 red sweet bell pepper, cut
    into strips

Place all of the above in a large bowl. Cover with poppy seed dressing and toss gently to coat. Marinate for several hours. Serve as an appetizer, or as a whole meal.

Poppy Seed House Dressing:

1 c. white sugar
2/3 c. white vinegar
1 T. salt

1 T. dry mustard
1 c. vegetable oil
2 T. poppy seeds

Place first 4 ingredients in a blender and blend. Drop by drop, add the oil until it is incorporated. Add the poppy seeds.

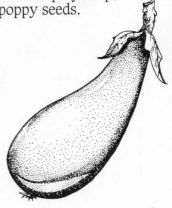

Lettuce is divine, although I'm not sure it is really a food.

—Diana Vreeland

Overnight Salad

Phyllis Laughrey
Mount Vernon, OH

Save time by preparing this easy salad the night before!

10-oz. carton frozen peas
1-1/2 c. mayonnaise
1/2 c. radishes, sliced
1/2 c. onion, chopped
1 head lettuce, torn
1 c. celery, chopped

1/2 c. green pepper, chopped
1 T. sugar
1 lb. bacon, cooked and
   crumbled
1/2 c. Cheddar cheese, shredded

Cook peas in boiling water for one minute. Drain and set aside to cool. Combine mayonnaise with radishes and onions; mix with peas. Place mayonnaise mixture in a large bowl, layer remaining ingredients in order listed. Top with bacon and cheese, cover and refrigerate overnight before serving.

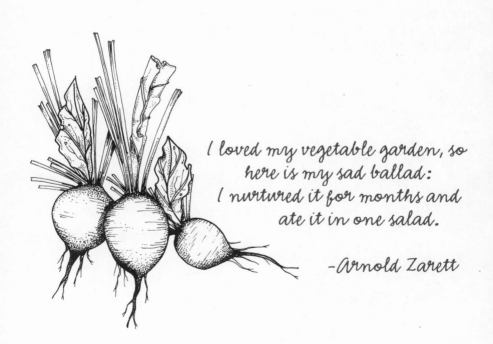

I loved my vegetable garden, so
here is my sad ballad:
I nurtured it for months and
ate it in one salad.

-Arnold Zarett

Caesar Salad

Vickie

*Our family likes this version, created from the traditional
Caesar salad recipe.*

3 cloves garlic, peeled and
    halved
4 thick slices Italian bread
5 T. olive oil
3 T. mayonnaise
3 T. lemon juice

1/4 t. salt
1/4 t. black pepper
1 head romaine lettuce, torn into
    pieces
1/4 c. Parmesan cheese, grated

Use 2 cloves of the garlic and rub the slices of bread on both sides.
Brush bread with 2 tablespoons of oil and cut into 1/2-inch cubes.
Spread cubes on an ungreased baking sheet and bake at 400 degrees
for 10 minutes, tossing occasionally, until golden brown and crisp. Rub
remaining garlic clove on the inside of a large chilled bowl. Combine
mayonnaise, lemon juice, salt, pepper and remaining 3 tablespoons oil;
whisk until smooth. Add romaine, Parmesan cheese, and croutons,
toss until well coated. Serves 4.

*Life is too short to bother with
tasteless tomatoes.*

–Cindy Pawlcyn

Chicken Salad

Rosemary Montgomery
High Bridge, NJ

My favorite recipe because it's so pretty and delicious, too!

6 boneless, skinless chicken
   breasts
1 T. fresh parsley, chopped
1 t. fresh dill, chopped
2 T. green pepper, chopped
2 T. celery, chopped

1/3 c. carrots, chopped
2/3 c. walnuts, chopped
1 t. black pepper
mayonnaise, to desired
   moistness
salt, to taste

Boil chicken until done, about 1-1/2 hours. Cut chicken into bite-size cubes. Combine chicken, parsley, dill, green pepper, celery, carrots, walnuts and crushed black pepper. Add mayonnaise to desired moistness and salt to taste. Refrigerate a few hours and serve in a decorative bowl lined with leaves of lettuce. Serves 4.

I want to go home to the dull old town, with the shaded street and the open square; and the hill and the flats and the house I love and the paths I know, I want to go home.

—Paul Kester

Family Reunion Fruit Salad

Debbie Cummons-Parker
Lakeview, OH

One of our family favorites. It was found in an old-fashioned church cookbook!

15-oz. can fruit cocktail
15-oz. can mandarin oranges
20-oz. can crushed pineapple

3-oz. pkg. instant vanilla
pudding mix

Drain fruits, reserving the syrup. Add pudding mix to the drained fruits and stir well. Add enough fruit syrup to moisten to desired consistency.

Summertime Salad

Margaret Scoresby
Mount Vernon, OH

There's nothing like fresh tomatoes from the garden for this recipe!

2/3 c. vegetable or olive oil
1/2 t. salt
1 garlic clove, minced
pepper to taste
1/4 c. salad vinegar

3 T. fresh basil, chopped
1/4 c. onion, chopped
1-1/2 c. mozzarella cheese cubes
1 pt. cherry tomatoes, halved

Prepare dressing by mixing first 5 ingredients well; toss in remaining ingredients. Chill until ready to serve.

Stencil a collection of Shaker boxes in country colors of barn red, mustard, moss green, and navy. Tuck some homemade cookies and your favorite recipe inside...perfect for a new neighbor!

Family-style
Casseroles

Hearing Mom's voice call us for dinner was always a welcome sound! We hopped out of the swing, dropped our bikes, or ran in from the barn as quickly as we could! It was always understood that Mom would prepare the dinner, and the kids would stay out of the kitchen until called on to fill water glasses, set the table, or bring an extra chair.

The aroma coming from the kitchen was always something special...a combination of sage, spices, chicken and biscuits; each of Mom's casseroles were a masterpiece!

The best part about gathering together for dinner was the company of extended family. Cousins, nephews, nieces, even dogs came to share in the fun, and there was always room at the table for new friends. That has always been the best part of family dinners; when family and friends get together to share.

Shepherd's Pie

Barbara Arnold
Toledo, OH

A truly old-fashioned dish. Try mashing your potatoes with sour cream and cream cheese...wonderful!

1 lb. ground beef
1/4 c. onion, chopped
1/2 t. salt
1 envelope brown gravy mix
10-oz. pkg. frozen peas and
  carrots

1-1/2 c. mashed potatoes,
  seasoned and warmed
1/2 t. dried basil leaves
1/4 c. Cheddar cheese, shredded

Cook ground beef and onion over medium high until meat is browned and onions are tender. Sprinkle with salt. Prepare gravy mix according to package directions and add to meat mixture. After gravy thickens, add frozen vegetables and basil. Cover and simmer for 5 minutes. Pour into 1-1/2 quart casserole. Fold cheese into mashed potatoes. Spoon into a ring on top of meat. Bake at 450 degrees for 15 minutes or until potatoes are lightly browned on top.

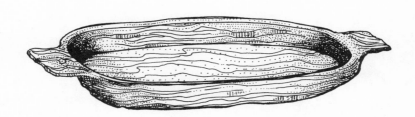

The golden rule of friendship is to listen to others as you would have them listen to you.

—David Augsburger

Shrimp with Garlic

Cheryl Bierley
Miamisburg, OH

This recipe is dear to me because it reminds me of the special occasions in my childhood. Mom would prepare this dish for family-birthdays, graduations and when our family was expecting company.It's a bit fancy, but quite simple to make.

1 c. butter, melted
2 cloves garlic, minced
1/3 c. parsley, chopped
1/2 t. paprika
dash cayenne pepper
1/2 c. cooking sherry or
    white wine

2 c. soft bread crumbs
5 to 6 c. shrimp, cleaned and
    cooked
Garnish: parsley, chopped

To melted butter add garlic, parsley, paprika, cayenne pepper and cooking sherry. Mix thoroughly. Add bread crumbs and toss. Place shrimp in an 11"x7"x1-1/2" baking dish. Spoon the butter mixture over the shrimp. Bake at 325 degrees for 25 minutes or until crumbs brown. Sprinkle additional chopped parsley over top before serving.

*Basically the only thing we need
is a hand that rests on our own,
that wishes it well,
that sometimes guides us.*

-Hector Biancíotti

Family-style Casseroles

Red Beans & Rice Casserole

Sandy Spayer
Jeromesville, OH

A hearty dish that will satisfy the whole family.

2 c. dried red kidney beans, sorted and rinsed
1 T. vegetable oil
8 oz. hot Italian sausage
1 lg. yellow onion, chopped
1 lg. sweet green pepper, chopped
1/2 c. celery, chopped
2 cloves garlic, minced
8 oz. smoked ham, diced

4 c. beef broth
2 bay leaves
1/2 t. dried thyme
1/2 t. dried marjoram
1/4 t. cayenne pepper
2 c. long-grain rice, cooked
1 T. red wine vinegar
1/2 t. salt
hot red pepper sauce, optional

Place beans in a 6-quart Dutch oven and cover with water; soak beans overnight. Drain beans and set aside. Heat oil in Dutch oven; add Italian sausage and sauté until brown. Remove and place on paper towels to drain. Remove all but 2 tablespoons of pan drippings. Combine onion, green pepper, celery and garlic and sauté until tender. Add reserved beans, ham, broth, bay leaves, thyme, marjoram and cayenne. Over high heat, bring ingredients to a boil. Reduce the heat to low and simmer, covered, until beans are tender, about 1-1/2 hours. Discard bay leaves. Drain bean mixture, reserving one cup liquid. Place bean mixture and reserved liquid into a lightly greased 3-quart casserole. Stir in rice, vinegar, and salt to taste. Bake covered 30 minutes. Serves 6.

Hang an old-fashioned wooden pitchfork by the back door...a handy hat rack!

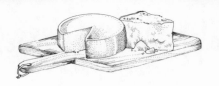

Chicken Tetrazzini

Debbie Musick
Yukon, OK

This recipe came from one of my mother's best friends: "Aunt" Cathryn. She always served it for holiday dinners and now my mother makes it for us. Each time we visit our mother, she serves it or has it in a casserole dish for us to take home and bake. I have wonderful memories of "Aunt" Cathryn; when we make this recipe, it brings her back for awhile.

1 lg. onion, minced
2 T. butter
2 10-3/4 oz. cans cream of
   mushroom soup
2 10-3/4 oz. cans cream of
   chicken soup
8-oz. pkg. Old English cheese
1/2 c. milk
1/2 c. water
1 t. curry powder

1/4 t. dried thyme
1/8 t. dried basil
1/4 t. dried oregano
2 7-oz. pkgs. spaghetti noodles,
   cooked
5-lb. chicken, cooked and cubed
4-oz. jar pimentos
salt and pepper to taste
Parmesan cheese, grated

Sauté onion in butter. Add soups, cheese, milk, water and spices. Add spaghetti to soup mixture, fold in chicken and pimentos. Spoon casserole into two, 13"x9" casserole dishes. Salt and pepper to taste, top with grated cheese. Bake at 350 degrees for 45 minutes.

Babies are always more trouble than you thought...and more wonderful.

-Charles Osgood

Steak 'n Potatoes

Anita McClard
Pelion, SC

I like this recipe because it's perfect for round steak and can easily be prepared in my slow cooker, too.

3 T. flour
salt and pepper to taste
3-lb. round steak
1 sm. onion, chopped
7 med. potatoes

2 10-3/4 oz. cream of
   mushroom soup
1 c. milk
4-1/2 oz. can button
   mushrooms

In a medium bowl, combine flour, salt and pepper. Cut round steak into 2-inch pieces, dip round steak in flour to coat. In a skillet, brown meat and onion in a small amount of shortening. Set aside. Peel and slice potatoes in 1/8-inch thick pieces. Boil for only 2 minutes. Mix mushroom soup with milk. Layer potatoes, steak, and soup mixture, ending with soup. Sprinkle with mushrooms. Bake in 300 degree oven for 2 hours. Serves 4.

The best things you can give children, next to good habits, are good memories.

-Sydney J. Harris

Onion & Cheese Casserole

Kristi Warzocha
Lakewood, OH

Combining sweet onions and cheese make this casserole delicious!

2 c. butter-flavored crackers,
   crushed and divided
1/2 c. butter, divided
3 lbs. onion, sliced
2 T. all-purpose flour
1/2 t. salt
1/2 t. ground black pepper

2 c. milk
1/2 lb. pasteurized processed
   cheese, diced
Garnish: sweet red pepper, cut
   into rings

Layer one cup cracker crumbs in a lightly oiled 11"x8" baking dish; set aside. In a skillet, melt 1/4 cup of butter. Stir in onions, cooking until tender. Spoon onions over cracker crumbs. Melt remaining 1/4 cup butter and stir in flour, salt, and pepper. Stir constantly and cook for one minute. Blend in milk gradually. Continue to stir well and cook until mixture is thick. Add cheese and stir until mixture is smooth. Pour over onions, sprinkle with remaining cracker crumbs. Bake at 350 degrees for 25 to 30 minutes or until lightly browned. Garnish with red pepper rings. Serves 12.

Life is like an onion, you peel it off one layer at a time, and sometimes you weep.

-Carl Sandburg

Baked Chicken & Wild Rice

Michele MacIntyre
Placerville, CA

Our family loves this because it tastes great and is so simple to prepare. We make it the night before and I just put it in the oven when I get home from work.

10-3/4 oz. can cream of chicken soup
10-3/4 oz. can cream of celery soup
1 pkg. dry onion soup mix
1 soup can of white or red wine
2 6-oz. boxes wild rice mix
4 skinless, boneless chicken breasts, cut into bite-size pieces

In a large bowl, combine soups, onion soup mix and wine. Mix together thoroughly. Add 2 packages of wild rice mix, do not use seasoning packets included in packages. Mix well. Place this rice mixture in a 13"x9" baking dish. Place chicken on top of rice mixture. Cover dish with foil and place in refrigerator overnight. Preheat oven to 350 degrees and cook for one to 2 hours or until chicken is thoroughly cooked. Serves 4 to 6.

Hang a small berry wreath on your cupboard doorknobs!

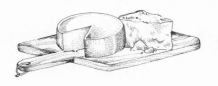

Spaghetti Pie

Eleanor Bierley
Miamisburg, OH

A great family meal; just add a salad and some garlic bread!

1/2 lb. spaghetti, cooked
2 eggs
1/4 c. Parmesan cheese
1/2 t. salt

1/4 lb. pepperoni
2 c. mozzarella cheese
2 c. spaghetti sauce

Combine spaghetti, eggs, Parmesan cheese, and salt. Mix thoroughly. Grease 13"x9" baking dish and place half of mixture in bottom. Layer top with half of pepperoni and mozzarella cheese. Then layer with remaining spaghetti mixture. Add remaining pepperoni and mozzarella cheese. Bake for 15 to 20 minutes at 350 degrees. Cut in squares and serve topped with sauce.

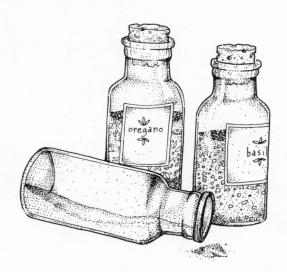

It's a comfort to always find pasta in the cupboard and garlic and parsley in the garden.

-Alice Waters

Down Home Tuna Casserole

Karen Urfer
New Philadelphia, OH

My family loves this creamy casserole! As the parents of two young children, my husband and I believe in the importance of sharing meals together. When I serve this casserole, everyone races to the table where we can sit as a family and share our blessings.

8-oz. pkg. noodles
2 T. butter
1 c. celery, chopped
1/4 c. onion, chopped
10-3/4 oz. can cream of
   mushroom soup
2 T. flour
3/4 c. milk

1/4 t. black pepper
1/4 t. thyme
9-1/4 oz. can tuna, drained and
   flaked
1 stack of round, buttery
   crackers, crushed
1/4 c. Parmesan cheese, grated

Cook noodles according to package directions and place in a 1-1/2 quart casserole dish. In a saucepan melt the butter and cook the celery and onions until tender. Add to the noodles. In a separate bowl, blend the soup, flour, milk, pepper and thyme. Blend well and add the tuna. Combine with the noodles and mix well. Combine the cracker crumbs with the Parmesan cheese and sprinkle over top. Bake at 350 degrees for 25 minutes.

Hang an old-fashioned red, white and blue bunting over your door!

Sour Cream Enchiladas

Pam Hilton
Centerburg, OH

Always a favorite when served with Spanish rice or beans!

2 10-3/4 oz. cans cream of
  chicken soup
1 c. sour cream
2 c. sharp Cheddar cheese,
  grated
4-1/2 oz. can chopped green
  chilies, undrained

1 sm. onion, diced
2 T. picante sauce
2 doz. corn tortillas
Garnish: lettuce, shredded and
  sour cream

Combine all ingredients except tortillas in a large saucepan. Heat and stir over low heat until cheese melts. Soften tortillas in very hot oil in frying pan, for a few seconds on each side. Drain on paper towels. Spoon 2 tablespoons of soup mixture onto a tortilla, roll, and place in baking dish. Continue with remaining tortillas. Pour remaining soup mixture over rolled tortillas and bake at 350 degrees for 25 to 30 minutes. Top with more cheese just before serving. Serve with shredded lettuce and sour cream.

Casserole: just another word for leftovers!

—Vinnie Tonellli

Mary's Noodle Bake

Mary Baker
Bayonet Point, FL

An easy casserole to prepare and perfect to share with neighbors.

16-oz. pkg. wide noodles
1-1/2 lb. ground beef
4 lg. onions, chopped
1 lb. mushrooms, sliced
4 stalks celery, chopped
1 green bell pepper, chopped

2 T. butter
3 10-3/4 oz. cans tomato soup
juice of half a lemon
1 lb. sharp Cheddar cheese,
  grated

Cook noodles according to package directions, set aside. Brown the ground beef and drain. Sauté the onions, mushrooms, celery and green pepper in butter. Combine remaining ingredients and fold in noodles. Bake at 350 degrees for one hour or until bubbly. Serves 10.

Search flea markets for primitive herb drying racks with swinging arms...perfect for displaying your homepsun kitchen towels!

Old-Fashioned Pork Chop Bake

Sue Martin
Delaware, OH

An easy one-dish recipe that we make ahead of time, refrigerate and put in the oven before our family arrives for dinner.

6 pork chops
salt and pepper to taste
1 med. onion, thinly sliced
3/4 c. rice, uncooked

1 green pepper, sliced into rings
28-oz. can peeled whole
   tomatoes, undrained
15-oz. can tomato sauce

Rinse pork chops and pat dry. Lightly salt and pepper both sides of each pork chop and place in a single layer in a baking pan which has been lightly coated with a cooking spray. Place one onion slice and 2 tablespoons of rice on each pork chop. Add one green pepper ring on top of each rice-topped pork chop. In a mixing bowl, combine whole tomatoes and tomato sauce. Pour over the top of pork chops, covering all rice. Cover and bake at 350 degrees for 1-1/2 hours. Serves 4 to 6.

Add a drawstring to old feed and sugar sacks and hang on a peg in the laundry room...great for sorting clothes!

Family·style Casseroles

Chicken & Green Bean Bake

Donna Lewis
Bellflower, CA

Perfect for a busy family...a quick recipe for your slow cooker!

2 or 3 skinless, boneless
    chicken breasts
salt
pepper
garlic powder

10-3/4 oz. can cream of
    mushroom soup
1/2 c. milk
14-1/2 oz. can green beans,
    drained
2.8-oz. can French fried onions

Place chicken breasts in crock pot. Season with salt, pepper and garlic powder to taste. Cook until done, approximately 2 to 3 hours on high. Drain off any liquid. Return chicken to pot. Add mushroom soup, milk, and green beans. Cover mixture with onions. Sprinkle with pepper. Cover and cook 30 minutes longer.

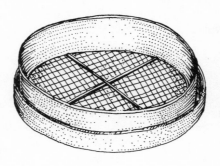

After a good dinner, one can forgive anybody, even one's own relatives.

-Oscar Wilde

Family Night Noodle Bake

LaRayne Cummons
Lakeview, OH

Set aside one night each week to spend just with family...go for a walk, play games or read a favorite book. This quick and easy casserole will let you spend more time together!

2 c. wide noodles
1 lb. ground beef
1/2 lb. ground pork
2 T. butter or margarine
2/3 c. onion, chopped
2   10-3/4 oz. cans condensed
    tomato soup
3-oz. pkg. cream cheese

2 T. sugar
1-1/2 T. Worcestershire sauce
1/4 t. pepper
1 t. salt
1 c. cornflake cereal, crushed
1/2 c. butter, melted

Cook noodles according to package directions; set aside. In a large skillet, combine meats and brown lightly in butter. Add onion and cook until tender, but not brown. Add soup, cheese, sugar, Worcestershire sauce and seasonings. Simmer for 15 minutes. Place noodles in a 11"x7" buttered baking dish. Pour sauce over noodles. Mix cereal with melted butter and sprinkle over the top. Bake at 350 degrees for 20 minutes or until heated through. Serves 8.

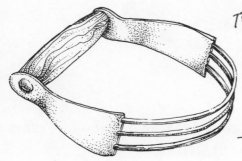

Treat your friends as you do your pictures, and place them in their best light.

–Jennie Jerome Churchill

Reuben Casserole

Phyllis Laughrey
Mount Vernon, OH

A favorite sandwich turned into a casserole!

2 16-oz. can sauerkraut,
    drained
2 12-oz. cans corned beef,
    crumbled
4 c. Swiss cheese, shredded

1 c. mayonnaise
1 c. Thousand Island dressing
4 T. butter
1/2 c. rye bread crumbs

Layer the above in a 13"x9" pan starting with sauerkraut, then the corned beef, then the cheese. Set aside while preparing sauce. Mix mayonnaise and dressing together, pour over casserole mixture. Mix together butter and bread crumbs. Sprinkle generously over top of all the above. Bake at 375 degrees for 30 minutes.

Display vintage linens, delicate lace, or embroidered pillowcases on an antique quilt rack.

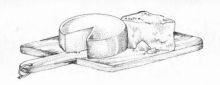

Chicken & Biscuits

Laura Fenneman
Lima, OH

Serve with a tall glass of milk and a crisp salad; delicious!

16-oz. pkg. mixed vegetables
10-3/4 oz. can cream of chicken
  soup
8-oz. can chopped chicken
1 c. tomatoes, chopped

1-1/2 c. Cheddar cheese,
  shredded
1-1/2 c. milk
1-1/2 c. biscuit mix
2.8-oz can French fried onions

Cook vegetables according to package directions. Combine vegetables with next 3 ingredients, one cup cheese and 3/4 cup milk. Put in greased 12"x8" baking dish. Cover and bake at 375 degrees for 15 minutes. Combine biscuit mix, 3/4 cup milk and 1/2 can onions. Mix thoroughly. Drop by spoonfuls to form 6 biscuits around edge of casserole. Bake uncovered until biscuits are light brown. Top with remaining cheese and onions and bake until cheese is completely melted and onions are toasted.

In the childhood memories of every good cook, there's a large kitchen, a warm stove, a simmering pot and a Mom.

-Barbara Costikyan

Ruth's Rice Casserole

Dorothy Baldauf
Crystal Lake, IL

A recipe shared with me by a very dear friend.

6 T. margarine
1 c. long-cooking rice
3/4 c. onion, diced
3/4 c. green pepper, diced

4-oz. can mushroom stems and
 pieces, drained
10-3/4 oz. can chicken and rice
 soup
1 soup can of water

Melt margarine in frying pan. Add rice and cook until rice is brown. Add onion, green pepper and mushrooms, browning until almost cooked. Pour into a 2-1/2 quart buttered casserole and add the chicken soup and water. Cover casserole and bake for 60 to 70 minutes at 350 degrees. This recipe can be served with beef, chicken or ham.

Spread a small coverlet on a child-size chair. Add a tin candle pan of wooden apples or dried oranges for a simple welcome.

Turkey Casserole

Anne Marie Wherthey
Tulsa, OK

My family enjoys this dish because it's so tasty, I enjoy it because it's easy to prepare!

1/2 c. celery, diced
1/2 c. onion, diced
2 T. butter
2 c. cooked turkey, diced
1/2 c. black olives, sliced

1/2 c. chicken broth
10-3/4 oz. can cream of chicken soup
Italian-style croutons

Sauté celery and onion in butter, add turkey and olives. Combine broth with soup and blend with turkey mixture. Add additional broth if needed to thin mixture. It should not be thick, but resemble soup. Pour into a one-quart buttered casserole dish. Top with croutons and bake at 375 degrees for 30 minutes. Serve over rice or wide noodles. Serves 6.

Home is heaven for beginners.

-Charles H. Parkhurst

Family·style Casseroles

Southwestern Chicken

Joanne West
Beavercreek, OH

Great for family reunions or neighborhood block parties!

1 t. salt
1/2 t. ground black pepper
1/4 t. garlic powder
1-1/2 lbs. boneless, skinless
   chicken breasts, cubed
1/4 c. butter
1 c. fresh cilantro leaves, finely
   chopped

3-1/2 c. fresh broccoli flowerets
1 lb. processed cheese, diced
10-oz. can diced tomatoes with
   green chilies
4 c. rice, cooked
Garnish: sour cream

Combine salt, pepper and garlic powder well and sprinkle evenly over chicken. Heat butter in a large skillet, stir in cilantro and chicken. Cook for 10 minutes, stirring occasionally. Add broccoli and continue cooking until broccoli is tender and chicken juices run clear. Remove from heat and set aside. Combine cheese, tomatoes and green chilies in a saucepan and cook over low heat until cheese melts. Remove from heat and set aside. Spoon rice into a greased 2-1/2 quart casserole; top with chicken mixture. Pour cheese mixture over chicken, cover and bake at 350 degrees for 25 to 30 minutes. Serves 6 to 8. Garnish with sour cream.

A man travels the world over in search of what he needs and returns home to find it.

-George Moore

Scalloped Tomato Casserole

Ann Magner
New Port Richey, FL

This recipe is over 100 years old!

6 slices bacon, diced
1/2 c. celery, chopped
1/2 c. onion, chopped
28-oz. can tomatoes, undrained
   and broken up
4 slices bread, torn into pieces

1 T. brown sugar
1/2 t. salt
1/2 t. summer savory
1/4 t. pepper
2 T. butter
2 T. Parmesan cheese, grated

In large skillet, cook bacon until crisp. Set aside and drain all but 2 tablespoons of drippings. Stir in celery and onion, sauté until tender. Add remaining ingredients, except butter and cheese, blend well. Place mixture into a lightly oiled 1-1/2 quart baking dish. Dot with butter and sprinkle with cheese. Bake 30 minutes at 350 degrees.

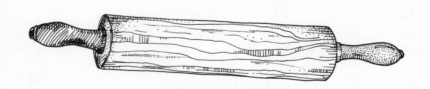

Recall it as often as you wish, a happy memory never wears out.

-Libbie Fudim

Apple Valley Squash Casserole

Rebecca Norris
Apple Valley, MN

As far as our family knows, my grandmother created this recipe...without any specific measurements!

4 or 5 med. yellow squash,
   peeled and chopped
2 T. butter or margarine
1/2 c. sugar

1 egg, beaten
1/4 lb. saltine crackers, crushed
nutmeg
black pepper

Cover squash with water in a medium saucepan and cook until tender. Drain. Add margarine to squash in pan and mash with a potato masher until relatively smooth. Add sugar and egg. Mix. Add enough cracker crumbs to make mix about the consistency of cornbread batter. Pour into a buttered pie plate and sprinkle top with nutmeg and black pepper. Bake in a 350 degree oven for approximately 25 minutes or until lightly brown on top and around edges. Serve hot.

A collection of sterling-silver tea balls is beautiful nestled in an old porcelain bowl.

Chicken King Casserole

Wendy Lee Paffenroth
Pine Island, NY

We serve this with a salad or coleslaw and warm bread. It's quick,
great for leftover chicken and gone in one sitting...my family loves it!

6 boneless chicken breasts
4 oz. bowtie pasta
10-3/4 oz. can cream of broccoli
   soup
10-3/4 oz. can creamy chicken
   mushroom soup
4-oz. can mushroom stems and
   pieces, drained and rinsed
1/2 c. milk

16-oz. carton sour cream
1 c. frozen peas
1 sleeve saltine crackers,
   crushed
2 T. butter, melted
1/4 t. dried parsley
1/4 t. garlic powder
1/4 t. salt
1/4 t. celery seed

Boil chicken until thoroughly cooked, cut up and place in a large
mixing bowl, set aside. Cook pasta according to package directions,
drain and rinse. In a medium mixing bowl, whisk together soups,
mushrooms, milk, sour cream and peas. Combine crackers and butter
well. Spread 3/4 of the cracker mixture over the bottom of a
13"x9" baking dish. Layer chicken, pasta and spices. Pour soup
mixture over pasta layer, sprinkle with reserved cracker mixture. Bake
at 350 degrees for 30 to 40 minutes or until thoroughly heated.

A dog wags its tail with its heart.

-Martin Buxbaum

Hometown
Main Dishes

I can still recall my mother telling me, "Don't get your Sunday clothes dirty, we'll be leaving any minute!" I knew if I behaved, I could bring a friend home for dinner and we could play all afternoon. After services were over, the members would visit outside awhile and then go home.

My friend and I would sit on the back steps playing jacks and getting more and more hungry by the minute! After what seemed like forever, Mom would call us in for dinner!

We'd take our places at the table and Dad would say the blessing. We'd then anxiously pass around plates of fried chicken, mashed potatoes and gravy, corn on the cob, warm rolls and icy lemonade. Sunday dinner was a special occasion at our house; everyone talking and laughing at the same time.

After dinner my friend and I would play outside, swing in the tree or take a bike ride; reluctant for the day to end.

Country Porkchops

Crystal Lappie
Worthington, OH

This recipe came from my kitchen creativity...a little of this and a little of that! It's my favorite recipe because it's so simple to prepare and delicious! The meat is so tender it can be cut with a fork.

4 to 6 pork chops   1/2 c. butter, melted
16-oz. box herb stuffing mix

Place pork chops in a shallow baking dish and bake uncovered at 250 degrees for one hour. Prepare the herb stuffing mix according to the box directions. Remove cooked porkchops from the oven and layer the stuffing mix on each porkchop, spoon on melted butter. Place back in the oven for an additional 15 to 20 minutes. Serves 4 to 6.

Use it up, wear it out; make it do, or do without.

—New England Proverb

One-Pot Supper

Wendy Lee Paffenroth
Pine Island, NY

A favorite in our family and the whole meal can be prepared in less than 30 minutes! We like it best served with salad and corn muffins.

8-oz. pkg. egg noodles
1-1/2 lbs. ground beef
1/2 c. onion, chopped
10 1/2-oz. can cream of
   mushroom soup
3/4 c. milk
1/8 t. pepper

1 t. parsley, chopped
8-oz. pkg. light cream cheese,
   cut up in pieces
16-oz. can of whole kernel corn,
   rinsed and drained

Cook egg noodles according to package directions; set aside. In a heavy Dutch oven, brown the meat and the onion. Drain off any grease. Mix in the mushroom soup and the milk and stir well until blended. Add pepper, parsley and cream cheese. Keep stirring until the cream cheese is melted. Add the corn. When ready to serve, spoon over egg noodles. Serves 4.

Wisdom doesn't necessarily come with age. Sometimes age just shows up all by itself.

—Tom Wilson

Sloppy Joes

Pat Decker
N. Muskegon, MI

Our family still thinks these are the best...tangy, rather than spicy.

1 lb. ground beef
10-3/4 oz. can tomato soup
1/2 green pepper, diced
2 T. vinegar

1 t. sugar
1 sm. onion, diced
2 T. Worcestershire sauce

Brown ground beef in a medium saucepan and drain. Add the remaining ingredients to the beef. Simmer on low heat for 30 to 60 minutes, until heated through.

Colonial Dinner

Kendra Landry
Mancelonia, MI

An old-fashioned, family dinner.

6 pork chops
3 T. oil
1 c. celery, chopped
1 orange, thinly sliced

2 c. cranberries, chopped
1/4 c. sugar
1/4 c. brown sugar
salt and pepper to taste

Sauté pork chops in oil until browned. Remove from saucepan and sauté celery and orange slices for 5 to 10 minutes. Return pork chops to saucepan, top with cranberries, sugars and salt and pepper. Cover and simmer 30 minutes. Turn pork chops and continue to simmer an additional 30 minutes. Serves 4 to 6.

Frame the pages of an old vintage scrapbook to make a wonderful wall display!

Pork & Sauerkraut Supper

Karen Mohn
Bethel, PA

We love this recipe because it's wonderful when we combine it with mashed potatoes and fresh ingredients grown on our farm!

6 pork ribs, country-style
2 T. oil
1 med. onion, diced
1 c. apple juice

2 lbs. sauerkraut, drained
2 apples, diced
2 t. brown sugar
salt and pepper to taste

Brown pork in oil. Remove from pan. Cook onion in drippings until tender. Stir in 1/4 cup apple juice. In large covered roaster, combine onion, drippings, sauerkraut, apples, sugar and remaining apple juice. Tuck pork into kraut and sprinkle with salt and pepper. Cover and bake at 350 degrees for 2 hours, basting occasionally.

A stack of vintage luggage found in an old attic, can make a terrific end table or nightstand.

Smothered Steak

Stephanie Quincy
Iola, KS

An old-fashioned recipe...great with roasted corn!

3/4 c. milk, separated
1/2 c. flour
4 sm. round steaks, tenderized
4 T. oil

1 sm. yellow onion, diced
10-3/4 oz. can cream of
   mushroom soup
salt and pepper to taste

Place 1/4 cup milk and flour in separate bowls. Dip steak in milk then dredge in flour on both sides. Brown steaks in oil on both sides; place in casserole dish. Sauté onion until tender, add soup and remaining milk. Simmer until gravy thickens and pour over steak. Bake, covered, for 45 minutes at 350 degrees. Remove lid and bake an additional 15 minutes.

Nobody can do for little children what grandparents do. Grandparents sort of sprinkle stardust over the lives of little children.

-Alex Haley

Grandma's Yankee Fried Chicken

Natalie Giberson
Keflavik, Iceland

A great old recipe that's been handed down for years!

6 boneless chicken breasts
3 eggs, beaten

1/2 c. butter
1-1/2 c. bread crumbs

Boil chicken until juices run clear when pricked with a fork. Set aside to cool. Beat eggs in bowl. Set aside. In large skillet, melt butter on low heat. Cut chicken breasts into several pieces and dip in egg mixture, roll in bread crumbs. Fry chicken in butter, turning every few minutes until golden brown. Place on plate with paper towel to remove any excess butter.

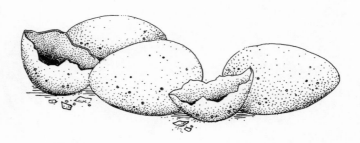

That is the best...to laugh with someone because you both think the same things are funny.

–Gloria Vanderbilt

Easy Stroganoff

Kathy Williamson
Delaware, OH

Quick to make for a family on the go!

1 lb. ground beef
1 sm. onion, chopped
10-3/4 oz. can cream of chicken
    soup

8-oz. carton sour cream
rice or noodles

Brown ground beef and onion, drain. Combine soup and one can of hot water. Simmer over low heat for one hour, until most of the liquid has cooked off. Just before serving, add sour cream. Serve over prepared rice or noodles.

For the laughter of children who tumble barefooted and bareheaded in the summer grass...our prayer of thanks.

—Carl Sandburg

Old-Fashioned Meatballs

Wendy Lee Paffenroth
Pine Island, NY

These are terrific because you can double the recipe and freeze them to use later. I wear a new pair of plastic cleaning gloves to roll the meatballs...less cleanup!

2 lbs. ground round
2 lg. eggs, beaten
2 t. Worcestershire sauce
1/4 c. catsup
1/4 c. onion, minced

1 t. dried oregano
1/8 t. black pepper
2 c. Italian seasoned bread crumbs

Place all ingredients in a large bowl and mix well. Combine all ingredients thoroughly and roll into meatballs. Place evenly on a cookie tray and bake at 325 degrees for about 30 minutes, drain oil. Cool and freeze in zipping freezer bags for future meals.

My father didn't tell me how to live; he lived, and let me watch him do it.

-Clarence Budington Kelland

Mom's Spaghetti Sauce

Jeannine Johnson-Tatum
Wauchula, FL

Every time I smell this sauce cooking, I can't help but think of Mom's dedication and determination to make everything she does the absolute best! This recipe is filled with Mom's timeless love!

1 sm. onion, diced
3 cloves garlic, chopped
1 T. butter
3 14-1/2 oz. cans tomatoes
3 6-oz. cans tomato paste
2 c. water
1/4 t. salt
1/2 t. pepper
1/2 t. dried basil

1/2 t. dried oregano
1/2 t. garlic powder
1/2 t. dried thyme
1 t. Italian seasonings
2 bay leaves
1 T. dried parsley
1/8 t. sugar
3 T. olive oil

Sauté onion and garlic in butter. Blend tomatoes and tomato paste in a blender until smooth. Combine with onion and garlic and spoon into a slow cooker. Gradually add the remaining ingredients. Cook on high for approximately 3 hours, stirring occasionally.

Old yelloware bowls are beautiful filled with apples, pomegranates, dried oranges, leaves or acorns.

Country Roast

Sandy Peterson
Glen Ellyn, IL

An easy roast to prepare and the gravy is wonderful served over mashed potatoes!

3-lb. beef roast
1 pkg. onion soup mix

10-3/4 oz. can cream of
mushroom soup

Place roast on heavy foil. Sprinkle dry soup mixture over roast, spread mushroom soup over top. Wrap tightly with foil. Bake at 325 degrees in roasting pan for 3-1/2 hours. To prepare gravy, add milk to pan drippings, stir well and heat through.

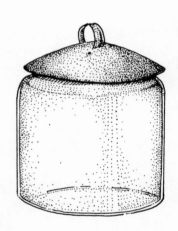

A sister is a gift to the heart, a friend to the spirit, a golden thread to the meaning of life.

—Anonymous

Chicken & Dumplings

Megan Pepping
Coshocton, OH

You can't go wrong with this homestyle dish! It's guaranteed to stick to your ribs!

4 lbs. chicken breasts
2 carrots, thinly sliced
2 celery stalks, thinly sliced
1 onion, chopped

1/2 t. dried rosemary
1-1/2 t. dried thyme
2 t. salt
1/2 t. pepper

Rinse chicken breasts and place in a large stockpot. Cover with water. Add carrots, celery, onion, rosemary, thyme, salt and pepper. Bring to a boil. Reduce to a simmer. When chicken is cooked, approximately 30 to 45 minutes or until juices run clear when chicken is pierced, remove from pot and shred. Return to broth.

Dumplings:

2 c. flour
3 t. baking powder
1 t. salt

2 T. parsley, minced
4 T. shortening
3/4 to 1 c. milk

Combine flour, baking powder, salt and parsley in a bowl. Cut in shortening until mixture resembles coarse meal. Add milk and stir briefly with a fork. If necessary, add additional milk to make dough hold together. Drop mixture by spoonfuls on top of boiling chicken mixture. Cover and steam for 20 minutes without lifting the lid. Don't even peek!

When I was younger, I could remember anything;
whether it happened or not.

– Mark Twain

Double-Crust Chicken Pot Pie

Margaret McNeil
Memphis, TN

*Delicious, tender chicken pot pie...
a true comfort food that's easy to prepare.*

2 9-inch refrigerated pie crusts
5-oz. can boneless chicken in
  broth, undrained, chopped
16-oz. can mixed vegetables,
  drained

10-3/4 oz. can cream of chicken
  soup
1/2 t. celery flakes
1/4 t. pepper
1/4 t. poultry seasoning

Place one refrigerated pie crust into a 9" pie plate according to package directions; do not bake. Combine remaining ingredients together and spoon into pie crust. Place second crust on top, fold edges under and flute. Cut slits in top. Bake at 400 degrees for 45 to 50 minutes. Let stand 10 minutes before serving.

*There's nothing half so pleasant
as coming home again.*

-Margaret Sangster

Meatloaf

Dee Rogers
S. Charleston, WV

Family-style meatloaf with a special sauce.

1-1/2 lbs. lean ground beef
1 c. tomato juice
3/4 c. oats
1 egg or 2 egg whites, beaten

1/4 c. onion, chopped
1/4 c. green pepper, chopped
1/2 t. salt
1/4 t. pepper

Heat oven to 350 degrees. Combine all ingredients and mix lightly. Press into 8"x4" loaf pan. Spoon piquant sauce over the meatloaf and bake for one hour. Drain and let stand for 5 minutes. Serves 6.

Piquant Sauce:

3 T. brown sugar
1/4 c. catsup

1/4 t. nutmeg
1 t. dry mustard

Mix together and spoon over meatloaf.

Cut a primitive star shape from an old piece of wood and paint it an old-fashioned color. When dry, twine a length of grapevine around and hang on your barn or milkhouse door!

Barbecued Pork Chops

Mary Marshall
Johnstown, PA.

Of all my mom's great meals, this was her best. When I make her recipe for my family and smell that wonderful aroma, I can close my eyes and see her face.

8 pork chops
3 T. vegetable oil
1/2 c. catsup
1 t. salt
1 t. celery seed

1/2 t. nutmeg
1/3 c. vinegar
1 c. water
1 bay leaf

Brown chops in hot oil. Combine remaining ingredients and pour over pork chops. Cover and bake at 325 degrees for 1-1/2 hours. Serves 8.

Display old-fashioned kitchen utensils in a favoite basket lined with homespun.

Mom's Lazy Lasagna

*Kimberly Nuttall
San Marcos, CA*

Making this lasagna recipe always brings to mind special occasions in my home.

1 lb. ground beef
2 28-oz. cans tomatoes
8-oz. can tomato sauce
1/4 t. garlic salt
1 envelope spaghetti sauce mix
1 c. ricotta or cottage cheese
1 egg

1/2 c. Parmesan cheese, grated
8-oz. pkg. lasagna noodles
6-oz. pkg. mozzarella cheese, shredded

Brown meat in large saucepan pan; drain. Add next 4 ingredients. Bring to a boil and simmer for 10 minutes. In a small bowl, mix ricotta or cottage cheese, egg and Parmesan cheese. Put a little of the meat sauce in bottom of a 13"x9" baking dish and alternate layers as follows: noodles, 1/3 of meat sauce, half of cheese mixture. Repeat and then top with remaining meat sauce. Sprinkle mozzarella cheese on top and cover with foil. Bake at 350 degrees for one hour or until noodles are tender. Let stand 10 minutes before cutting. Serves 8 to 10.

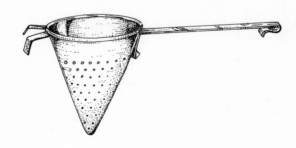

Life is a combination of magic and pasta.

-Federico Fellini

Grandma's Stuffed Cabbage

Karen Pungaew
Riverside, CA

*This recipe is special to me because it belongs to my Grandma Ponto.
She was not only the best grandma, but she was also the best cook.
When we were little we would cook all sorts of wonderful things, but
the best recipe she had was stuffed cabbage. We always made
it at Christmastime.*

1 sm. onion, diced	1 c. rice
2 T. oil	4-lb. head of cabbage
2 lbs. pork shoulder, ground	14-oz. can sauerkraut
salt and pepper to taste	1 pt. tomatoes, chopped

Sauté onion in oil, add meat and seasonings. Rinse rice thoroughly and
add to meat mixture. Cut out the center core of the cabbage head and
put cabbage in boiling water. Leave cabbage in water just until leaves
begin to wilt. Remove leaves and set aside. Remove the vein in the
center of the leaves, without cutting through the leaves. Spoon
2 tablespoons of meat mixture on each leaf. Roll up filled leaves,
pushing both ends in tightly. Repeat with remaining wilted cabbage
leaves. Any remaining cabbage can be chopped and lined inside the
bottom of a Dutch oven. On top, layer 1/2 of the sauerkraut, stuffed
cabbage rolls and remaining sauerkraut. Pour on tomatoes, adding
enough water to cover all. Bring to a boil, then reduce heat to low.
Simmer for 15 minutes. Makes 20 cabbage rolls.

*Memory is more indelible
than ink.*

-Anita Loos

Chicken Cacciatora

Mildred Panfile
Bayville, NJ

When we were on vacation in Long Island, New York, a wonderful Italian restaurant made this dish and I just had to learn how to make it! By trial and error, I did learn and now I've been making it for our family for more than 20 years.

4 lbs. chicken, cut into pieces
1/2 c. flour
1 t. salt
1 t. pepper
1/2 c. oil
1/4 c. onion, chopped
2 cloves garlic, finely chopped

1/2 c. carrots, chopped
1 T. dried parsley
1 bay leaf
1 t. dried basil
4 c. plum tomatoes, strained
1/4 c. red or white wine

Dredge chicken in flour, sprinkle with salt and pepper and brown in hot oil until golden brown on all sides. Place in covered dish and keep warm. Brown onions, garlic, carrots, parsley, bay leaf and basil in oil left in pan. Add tomatoes to onion mixture.
Bring to a boil. Add chicken and wine, simmer 30 minutes or until chicken is tender. Serve with prepared rice or angel hair pasta.

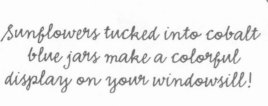

Sunflowers tucked into cobalt blue jars make a colorful display on your windowsill!

Farm-Fresh Spinach Quiche

Margaret Sloan
Westerville, OH

Use farm-fresh eggs for this recipe!

1 refrigerated pie crust
8 slices bacon, crisply cooked
    and crumbled
1/2 lb. Monterey Jack cheese,
    grated

3 eggs, beaten
1-1/2 c. milk
1 T. flour
10-oz. pkg. frozen spinach,
    thawed and drained

Lay pie crust in pie pan. Add 4 slices of crumbled bacon to bottom of pie crust. Mix cheese, eggs, milk, flour and spinach together. Pour over crust. Sprinkle 4 pieces of crumbled bacon on top. Bake at 350 degrees for one hour or until center is set.

Old-fashioned canning jars make perfect canisters for your country kitchen!

Pepper Steak

Mary Alice Foster
Reynoldsburg, OH

This wonderful recipe brings back such lovely memories! Memories of my brothers and sisters, our father coming in from the barn; stomping the snow off his boots, and our mother who had to stretch pennies into dollars. We were Depression Era kids, but the warmth and love in our home made us rich beyond belief. We always teased our father that he came in early from the barn when he knew we were having this dish!

1 lb. round steak, fat trimmed
1 T. oil
1/4 c. onion, chopped
1 garlic clove, minced
1 cube beef bouillon
3/4 c. boiling water
1/8 t. pepper

14-1/2 oz. can stewed tomatoes
1 med. green pepper, cut into
　strips
1/4 c. cold water
2 T. cornstarch
2 t. soy sauce

Cut round steak into 2-inch strips. Add oil to skillet and brown for 10 minutes. Add onion and garlic; cook for 3 to 4 minutes. Dissolve bouillon cube in 3/4 cup boiling water and pour into skillet. Sprinkle meat with pepper. Cover and simmer for 35 to 40 minutes, or until meat is tender. Add tomatoes and green pepper; cover and simmer for 10 minutes. Combine 1/4 cup cold water, cornstarch and soy sauce. Stir into skillet. Bring to a boil, and stir for 2 minutes. Serve over rice or noodles. Serve 4 to 6.

There is no spectacle on earth more appealing than that of a beautiful woman in the act of cooking dinner for someone she loves.

-Thomas Wolfe

Deep Dish Vegetable Pie

Vickie

Cut this pie into wedges and serve warm...delicious!

Crust:

1 pkg. active dry yeast
2/3 c. warm water
2 c. all-purpose flour, divided
1/2 c. corn chips, finely crushed

1 T. sugar
2 t. onion, finely chopped
3/4 t. salt
2 T. vegetable oil

In a small bowl, dissolve yeast in water; set side. In another bowl, combine one cup of flour, corn chips, sugar, onion and salt; stir until well blended. Add yeast mixture and oil to dry ingredients. Stir until smooth. Add remaining flour; stirring until well blended. Roll dough out to a 13-inch diameter circle on a lightly floured surface. Press dough into the bottom and sides of a well-greased 9" springform pan. Cover with a cloth and let rise for 10 minutes. Prick bottom of crust with a fork. Bake at 375 degrees for 25 to 30 minutes or until golden brown.

Filling:

1 T. vegetable oil
1 T. butter
3 c. fresh broccoli flowerets
3 c. cabbage, shredded
2 c. zucchini squash, thinly
    sliced
3 onions, chopped

1-1/2 c. carrots, sliced
1 t. salt
1/2 t. black pepper, ground
1/4 t. garlic powder
1/4 t. chili powder
1-1/2 c. sharp Cheddar cheese,
    shredded

In a large skillet, heat oil and butter over medium heat. Add next 9 ingredients, stirring constantly. Cook until vegetables are crisp-tender. Spoon over warm crust and sprinkle with cheese. Bake at 375 degrees for 8 to 10 minutes, or until cheese is melted. Serves 10.

Beef Brisket with Ginger Gravy

Teri Lindquist
Gurnee, IL

The only difficult part of of making this recipe is waiting for it to be ready! We serve this on buns for easy sandwiches or with mashed potatoes and carrots for dinner.

2 pkgs. dry onion soup mix
2 c. water
8 to 10-lb. beef brisket

12-oz. bottle chili sauce
10 ginger snap cookies

Pour dry onion soup mix into bottom of a large roasting pan. Pour in water and stir to combine. Place brisket into pan and cover meat with chili sauce. Break cookies into pieces and sprinkle around meat. Cover tightly and bake at 350 degrees for 1-1/2 hours. Check occasionally and add more water if necessary. Remove meat from pan and thinly slice. Return sliced meat to pan and spoon sauce over meat. Cover and cook another hour. Then turn heat down to 250 degrees and cook another 2 to 3 hours until meat is very tender. Serves 8 to 10.

Vintage toy trucks make fun utencil or napkin holders!

Stuffed Peppers

Dorothy Foor
Jeromesville, OH

A homestyle dish with a twist.

4 med. green peppers
4 slices bacon, cut into 2-inch
    pieces
1 c. scallions, chopped
2 c. frozen corn kernels, thawed
1/4 c. pimentos, chopped
3 T. fresh cilantro, chopped

1 sm. jalapeno pepper, chopped
1-1/4 t. chili powder
1-1/4 t. cumin, ground
1/2 t. salt
1 c. Monterey Jack cheese,
    shredded
1/4 c. tortilla chips, crushed

Slice 1/2 inch off the top of each pepper, remove stem from top, chop and reserve. Remove seeds from peppers and rinse well with cool water. Blanch peppers 5 minutes in boiling water. Remove and set on paper towels. Cook bacon until crisp and set aside to drain oil. Leave 2 tablespoons bacon drippings in the skillet. Sauté chopped pepper in bacon drippings until soft. Stir in scallions and sauté with peppers for 2 minutes. Add corn, pimentos, cilantro, jalapeno, chili powder, cumin and salt; stir and cook 3 minutes more. Remove from heat and stir in reserved bacon and 3/4 cup of Monterey Jack cheese. Spoon an equal amount of corn mixture into peppers. Place peppers in an ungreased 1-1/2 quart baking dish and bake uncovered at 350 degrees for 30 minutes. Toss crushed tortilla chips with the remaining cheese and place one tablespoon on top of each stuffed pepper. Continue to bake until cheese is melted. Serves 4.

Some wives do wonderful things with leftovers...
they throw them out!

—Anonymous

Swiss Steak

Betty Stout
Worthington, OH

If you have a busy family or a full day planned, make this hearty dish even easier! Brown the meat and place it in a slow cooker, top with the remaining ingredients and place on the low setting. Enjoy a day at the park or beach and come home to a terrific meal in 8 to 10 hours!

1/4 c. flour
1/2 t. salt
1/8 t. pepper
2-lb. round steak, cut into
    serving-size pieces
2 T. vegetable oil

28-oz. can tomatoes, undrained
    and broken up
1 rib celery, chopped
1 med. onion, sliced
1 T. bottled steak sauce

In shallow dish, combine flour, salt and pepper. Coat both sides of steak pieces with mixture. In large skillet, brown steak in oil. Remove from pan, drain excess fat. Return steak to skillet. Add remaining ingredients and bring to a boil. Reduce heat, cover and simmer for 1-1/2 to 2 hours or until tender. If desired, thicken gravy with additional flour dissolved in a small amount of water.

Show off your display of homespun kitchen towels in your favorite stoneware mixing bowl!

Chicken & Stuffing

Debbie Keady
Amsterdam, NY

You'll be asked for the recipe after friends taste this delicious dish!

2 to 4 boneless chicken breasts
10-3/4 oz. can cream of chicken
   soup
1/4 c. milk
1/4 c. chicken broth

6-oz. box chicken-flavored
   stuffing mix
4 T. butter, melted
1/2 c. chicken broth
Parmesan cheese, grated

Place chicken breasts in a Dutch oven, cover with water and cook until juices run clear when pierced with a fork. Drain, reserving broth; set aside. Cut chicken in small pieces and place in 1-1/2 quart greased baking dish. Combine soup, milk and broth. Pour over chicken. Combine stuffing seasoning mix packet, butter, and broth. Stir in dry stuffing and sprinkle on top of soup mixture. Cover and bake at 350 degrees for 30 minutes. Sprinkle with grated Parmesan cheese before serving. Serves 4 to 6.

After dinner sit awhile, after supper walk a mile.

-Anonymous

Layered Cabbage Rolls

Debbie Cummons-Parker
Lakeview, OH

The traditional meal we love, with a recipe that's half the work!

1 med. head cabbage, sliced or
   chopped
1-1/2 lb. ground beef
1/2 lb. sausage
1 sm. onion, chopped
1/4 c. green pepper, chopped
1 t. chili powder
1/4 t. garlic powder

1/2 t. salt
1/8 t. pepper
2/3 c. long-cooking rice,
   uncooked
2 10-3/4 oz. cans cream of
   tomato soup
2 cans water
2 T. brown sugar

Lightly oil a 13"x9" glass baking dish. Do not use a metal pan. Layer cabbage on bottom of pan. Brown ground beef, sausage, onion and green pepper. Drain oil. Add seasonings and rice to meat mixture, spread over cabbage. Mix together soup, water and brown sugar and pour over ingredients. Cover and bake at 350 degrees for 1-1/2 hours.

If six cooks followed the same recipe, the finished dish would vary six times.

-Theodora Fitzgibbon

Quick Chili Mac

Letty Lee Powers
Lakeview, OH

This is a quick, nutritious meal for the family on the go!

1 c. macaroni
1 green pepper, chopped
1 lg. onion, chopped
2 T. margarine
1 lb. ground beef

10-3/4 oz. can tomato soup
16-oz. can kidney beans
1/2 t. salt
1/2 t. chili powder

Prepare macaroni as directed on package. Drain and set aside. Sauté green pepper and onion in margarine until transparent. Add ground beef and brown. Add tomato soup, kidney beans, salt and chili powder. Simmer over low heat for 20 minutes. Add macaroni and heat through. Serves 4.

Old, rusty cookie cutters make whimsical windchimes outside your kitchen window!

Country Sides

Early in the morning we'd walk across the dewy grass to the garden to see if any of the early vegetables were ready to pick. There was always something exciting about going between the rows and discovering a bounty of fresh vegetables!

We'd fill our baskets to overflowing and then head back to the farmhouse. Mom had set chairs under our old shade tree and we'd sit together and shell peas, snap beans or husk corn. We'd then gather our vegetables together and go to the summer kitchen where they were quickly blanched and packed for the freezer.

We never picked so many that it became a chore, and many times friends or relatives were there to share the work. Afterward we'd sit down together for dinner, sampling some of our freshly-picked vegetables...green beans and new potatoes, slices of bright red tomatoes and crisp homemade pickles. As the evening wore on, the song of the birds gave way to dancing fireflies and the sound of peepers. We'd watch and listen and grow sleepy.

Family-style Baked Beans

Delores Berg
Selah, WA

A great side dish our family loves served with warm corn bread.

2 c. navy beans
1-1/2 c. smoked ham, cubed
1 sm. onion, chopped
1-1/2 c. brown sugar

8-oz. can tomato sauce
1/2 t. salt
1/8 t. pepper

Soak beans overnight in cold water. Simmer beans until tender, about one hour. Drain. Heat oven to 300 degrees. Place beans, ham and onion in bean pot. Combine brown sugar, tomato sauce and seasonings. Pour over beans. Add enough cold water to cover. Cover and bake for 5-1/2 to 6 hours. Serves 8.

Simplicity is the essence of happiness.

-Cedric Bledsoe

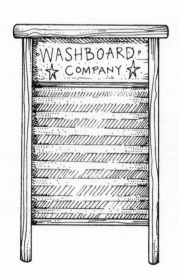

Ham & Cauliflower Au Gratin

Tiffany Moore
Grants Pass, OR

One of my favorite recipes because I know that my kids will eat their veggies without complaining!

2 10-oz. pkgs. frozen
  cauliflower, thawed and
  drained
1-1/4 c. smoked ham, cooked
  and chopped
10-3/4 oz. can condensed
  Cheddar cheese soup

1/4 c. milk
2/3 c. biscuit baking mix
2 T. butter
1/2 t. nutmeg
Garnish: parsley and paprika

Preheat oven to 400 degrees. Arrange cauliflower in ungreased 13"x9" baking dish. Sprinkle with ham. Combine soup and milk with hand beater until smooth, pour over ham. Mix remaining ingredients until crumbly. Sprinkle over soup mixture. Sprinkle with parsley and paprika, if desired. Bake until topping is golden brown, 20 to 25 minutes.

Wrap a bundle of dried herbs from your kichen garden in a vintage handkerchief...a perfect hostess gift!

Country Sides

German Potato Salad

Calla Andrews
Long Beach, CA

German Potato Salad was one of my first cooking successes as a new bride. My husband and his family raved over this recipe!

6 lg. new potatoes
10 bacon slices, chopped
1 red onion, finely chopped
4 t. flour
1 T. sugar

salt and pepper
1/2 c. cider vinegar
1/2 c. water
1/4 c. fresh parsley, minced
1 t. celery seeds

Steam potatoes until tender, cool and peel. Thinly slice potatoes and transfer to large bowl. Cook bacon in heavy skillet over medium heat until crisp. Add onion; cook one minute. Stir in flour and sugar. Season with salt and pepper, stir. Mix vinegar and water then pour over bacon mixture. Stir until thickened. Pour over potatoes. Mix in parsley and celery seeds.

What small potatoes we all are, compared with what we might be!

–Charles Dudley Warner

Cowboy Beans

Tambry Gardner
Delaware, OH

Great with grilled hamburgers or hot dogs and fresh corn on the cob!

1 lb. ground beef, browned and
    drained
16-oz. can baked beans
16-oz. can kidney beans
2 c. onions

3/4 c. brown sugar
1 c. catsup
2 T. dry mustard
1/4 t. salt
2 t. vinegar

Mix all ingredients together in a crock pot. Cook on high one to
2 hours or until thoroughly heated.

*Add a collection of birdhouses and pie birds to the
shelves of your kitchen cupboard!*

Country Sides

Old-Fashioned Macaroni & Cheese

Kathy Schroeder
Riverside, CA

A wonderful comfort food, so smooth and creamy.

2 c. macaroni
2 T. shortening, melted
2 T. flour

salt and pepper
2-1/2 c. milk
3 c. sharp Cheddar cheese, grated

Cook macaroni according to package instructions. Mix together shortening and flour over low heat. Add salt and pepper to taste. Gradually add milk, stirring constantly. Warm over medium heat just until it starts to boil and thicken. Add mixture to Cheddar cheese and stir until smooth. Pour in macaroni, top with extra grated cheese and bake uncovered in a 350 degree oven for 30 minutes.

Many's the long night I've dreamed of cheese...
toasted, mostly.

–Robert Louis Stevenson

Sweet Potato Casserole

Cindy Henderson
Greenville, SC

This side dish has been a part of our meals for many years. My mother used to make it each year for Christmas dinner; now we gather at my house and I carry on the tradition. Whatever the reason for the occasion, no meal is complete without this.

3 c. sweet potatoes, mashed
1 c. sugar
1/2 t. salt
2 eggs

2-1/2 T. margarine, melted
1/2 c. milk
1 t. vanilla

Mix all ingredients together and pour into a greased baking dish.

Topping:

1 c. brown sugar
1 c. nuts, chopped

1/3 c. flour
2-1/2 T. margarine, melted

Blend all ingredients in a small bowl. Sprinkle on top of sweet potatoes in baking dish. Bake at 350 degrees for 30 to 35 minutes or until brown sugar melts. Recipe may be doubled or tripled.

Keep your favorite cookbooks close at hand tucked inside an old-fashioned market basket.

Country Sides

Luke's Favorite Potatoes

Mary-Sue Bartlett
Cedar Falls, IA

When I want to make something extra special for my son, Luke, this is the recipe I turn to.

8 or 9 potatoes, unpeeled
2 c. half-and-half
1/2 c. butter

1/2 T. salt
Cheddar cheese, shredded
Parmesan cheese, grated

In a large saucepan, cover potatoes with water and boil until tender. When completely cool, peel potatoes and shred into a large mixing bowl. In a small saucepan, mix and heat half-and-half, butter and salt until warm. Pour over shredded potatoes and mix well. Put in a buttered 2-quart casserole dish. Cover with a layer of Cheddar cheese and a layer of Parmesan cheese. Refrigerate overnight. Bake at 350 degrees for approximately one hour. Serves 8.

Potatoes are to food what sensible shoes are to fashion.

-Linda Wells

Creamy Broccoli Stuffing

Carol Shirkey
Canton, OH

A cheesy side dish your family will love.

10-oz. pkg. chopped broccoli, frozen
1-1/2 T. butter, melted
2-1/2 T. flour

3/4 c. milk
6-oz. box herbed stuffing mix
1/4 lb. processed cheese, sliced

Cook broccoli until tender. Make white sauce of butter, flour and milk. Cook until thickened. Prepare stuffing mix according to directions on package. Lightly oil a 2-quart casserole dish. Put a layer of broccoli in bottom of baking dish, layer cheese slices on top of broccoli. Spread a layer of white sauce on top of the cheese, and then add a layer of stuffing. Repeat layers as above, ending with stuffing. Bake uncovered at 350 degrees for 30 minutes.

The best way to cheer yourself up is to try to cheer someone else up.

-Mark Twain

Country Sides

Scalloped Potatoes

Mary Hanson
Centerville, WA

A special recipe to me because I received it from my mother-in-law shortly after I was married.

1/2 c. onions
1/2 c. butter
4 lbs. potatoes
salt and pepper to taste
2 c. sour cream
2 10-3/4 oz. cans cream of
   mushroom soup

2 10-3/4 oz. cans cream of
   celery soup
1-1/2 c. Cheddar cheese,
   shredded
1 c. cornflake cereal, crushed

Sauté onions in butter and set aside. Cover potatoes with water, boil until tender and cut up into bite-size chunks. Mix all ingredients, except cereal, with onions. Spread mixture into a casserole dish and bake 350 degrees for one hour. Sprinkle crushed cereal over top of casserole the last 15 minutes.

An old seed display crate looks wonderful white-washed and filled with herbs, rolled up homespun towels, or dried flowers tucked inside.

Special Supper Stuffing

Carol Bull
Delaware, OH

Some of my fondest memories have been made antiquing with two dear friends through our local Amish community. We spend the day looking for treasures that "need a home" and then have lunch at a wonderful family-style restaurant that features traditional Amish foods. This "one dish meal" reminds me of good friends and good times every time I serve it. It's wonderful served with homemade bread and cabbage slaw.

2 1-lb. loaves white bread
2 lbs. chicken breasts, poached
1/2 c. fresh parsley, minced
1 c. onion, chopped
3/4 c. celery, chopped
1 c. carrot, shredded
1-1/4 c. boiled potatoes, finely
    chopped

1 T. sage
1 t. thyme
1 t. pepper
5 eggs
12-oz. can evaporated milk
2-1/2 c. chicken broth

Preheat oven to 350 degrees. Cube bread and toast on cookie sheets for 15 minutes. Transfer to a very large mixing bowl. Shred and chop the chicken breast and add to the bread cubes. Mix in the vegetables and the seasonings. Toss. In a medium bowl, beat the eggs, milk and broth. Pour over the bread cube mixture and stir gently. The mixture will be very moist. Allow to stand for one hour. Transfer stuffing to an oiled 3-quart glass casserole dish. Bake dressing for 2 hours or until center puffs up and is golden brown. Serves 10 to 16.

To be capable of steady friendship or lasting love, are the two greatest proofs, not only of goodness of heart, but strength of mind.

—William Hazlitt

Macaroni Corn Casserole

Judy Kelly
St Charles, MO

I've made this recipe so many times at my children's request, that it has already become a tradition!

1 c. macaroni, uncooked
16-oz. can whole kernel corn, undrained

17-oz. can cream-style corn
1/2 c. margarine
4 oz. processed cheese

Preheat oven to 350 degrees. Mix the macaroni, whole kernel corn and cream-style corn in a baking dish. Microwave the margarine and cheese in a microwave-safe dish until melted. Add to the corn mixture. Bake for 45 minutes. Serves 6 to 8.

Happiness isn't something you experience: it's something you remember.

—Oscar Levant

Company Potatoes

Alice Monaghan
St. Joseph, MO

A homestyle, creamy potato casserole that's perfect with any meal!

1/2 c. milk
1/2 lb. American cheese
1/2 c. shortening
12 med. potatoes, boiled in
    jackets then sliced

1 green pepper, diced
1 onion, diced
4-oz. jar pimentos, diced
1 T. parsley flakes
salt and pepper to taste

In a medium saucepan, combine milk, cheese and shortening. Stir until melted and smooth. Place the potatoes, green pepper, onion and pimentos in a large bowl. Add parsley flakes, salt and pepper. Add the cheese sauce to this mixture and gently mix together. Place the mixture in a 3-quart baking dish. Cover with foil and bake for 40 to 50 minutes in a 400 degree oven.

There was a place in childhood, that I remember well, and there a voice of sweetest tone, bright airy tales did tell, and gentle words, and fond embrace, were given with joy to me, when I was in that happy place upon my mother's knee.

-Samuel Lover

Fruited Yams

Cindy Watson
Gooseberry Patch

This recipe is a good side dish any time of year, but it's especially comforting on blustery, autumn days!

2 med. yams
1 c. pineapple, chopped
1 banana, sliced
3/4 c. apple, chopped
1/4 c. raisins
1/3 c. apple juice

1 T. brown sugar, packed
1 t. lemon peel, grated
1 t. cinnamon
1/2 t. ginger
1/4 t. nutmeg

Heat oven to 350 degrees. Spray 13"x9" dish with non-stick cooking spray. Peel and cut yams into 1/4-inch slices. Layer half of the yams in dish. Mix pineapple, banana, apple and raisins. Spread half of the fruit mixture over yams. Repeat with remaining yams and fruit mixture. Mix remaining ingredients. Pour evenly over yams and fruit mixture. Cover and bake 50 to 60 minutes or until yams are tender. Serves 6.

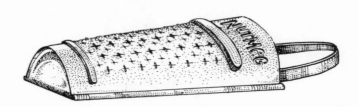

Set little terra cotta pots filled with fresh-growing herbs in a candlebox!

Overnight Potato Casserole

Jennifer Habush
Sherman Oaks, CA

I've make this dish every Thanksgiving and Christmas since 1977. I have never had the reputation of being a good cook, so my kind-hearted mother taught me how to make this delicious and easy recipe.

1/2 c. butter or margarine
10-3/4 oz. can cream of chicken
   soup
1-1/2 c. Cheddar cheese, grated

1 pt. sour cream
1/3 c. yellow onion, minced
2-lb. bag hash brown potatoes
1 c. breadcrumbs, buttered

Combine all ingredients, except hash browns, in a large saucepan. After mixture is heated through, add hash browns; mix well and heat again. Pour mixture into a 13"x9" buttered glass dish and top with one cup of buttered bread crumbs. Refrigerate overnight. Bake at 350 degrees for one hour or until golden and bubbly.

Let the sky rain potatoes!

-Shakespeare

Pickle Relish

Martha Riesterer
Castalia, OH

This dish was handed down to me from my Grandma. I remember making it was so much fun! We would set up the grinder outside on the picnic table and spend hours grinding the ingredients. Over the years this relish has become a cherished gift to family and friends.

8 qts. pickling cucumbers
salt
6 green peppers
6 red peppers
12 onions

2 bunches of celery
3 lbs. sugar
1 qt. vinegar
2 oz. mustard seed

Grind pickles and salt together, let sit overnight. Combine peppers, onions and celery; grind well and let sit overnight. In a large bowl, combine sugar, vinegar and mustard seed. Pour over well-drained pickles, blend with remaining ingredients. Heat through and immediately pour into sterilized jars, leaving 1/4-inch headspace. Add lids and rings. Process 10 minutes in a boiling-water canner. Makes 8 pints.

Jars nestled in an old tin tray, are perfect for holding dried herbs from your garden!

Vegetable Herb Trio

Dorothy Jackson
Weddington, NC

Every summer my family can hardly wait for the fresh vegetables to be harvested from the garden so we can prepare this recipe!

1/2 lb. green beans, cut into
   1-1/2 inch pieces
1/2 c. onion, chopped
2 T. fresh parsley, chopped
1 t. salt
3/4 t. fresh thyme
3/4 t. fresh sage

1/8 t. pepper
3/4 c. water
2 c. yellow squash, sliced
3 lg. tomatoes, cut into wedges
2 T. butter or margarine

Combine first 8 ingredients and 1/2 cup of water in a large skillet. Bring to a boil. Cover skillet, reduce heat and simmer for 10 minutes. Add squash and remaining water to skillet. Bring to a boil. Cover and reduce heat and simmer for another 10 minutes. Drain well. Add tomatoes and butter. Cook, stirring often, until butter melts. Serves 6.

Paint a folk art flag on the lid of your picnic basket!

Escalloped Corn

Carol Shirkey
Canton, OH

An old-fashioned corn dish that's so easy to make.

1/2 c. margarine
2 eggs
8-oz. carton sour cream
8-oz. can cream-style corn

8-oz. can whole kernel corn,
  undrained
8-oz. pkg. corn muffin mix

Preheat oven to 350 degrees. Melt margarine in a pan and pour into a bowl. Beat the eggs and add them to the margarine. Beat in sour cream, both cans of corn and muffin mix. Mix thoroughly. Put in a baking dish. Bake for one hour at 350 degrees.

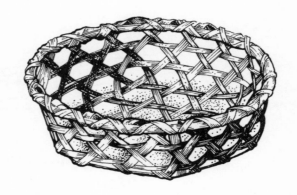

*Happiness makes up in height for what it
lacks in length.*

-Robert Frost

Copper Pennies

Cheryl Bierley
Miamisburg, OH

This side dish can be served hot or cold.

2 lbs. carrots, sliced
1 c. tomato sauce
1/4 c. margarine, melted
salt and pepper to taste
1/2 t. dry mustard

1 med. green pepper
1 c. sugar
1/2 c. vinegar
1/2 t. Worcestershire sauce
1 med. onion, diced

Cook carrots until tender, drain well and set aside. In a saucepan, combine remaining ingredients and cook 5 minutes over medium heat. Pour over carrots. Refrigerate at least 2 days to marinate. This dish can be served hot or cold, as a vegetable or relish.

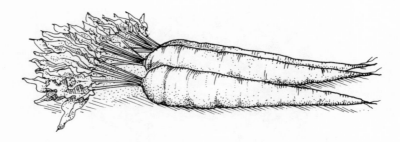

Some people may still have their first dollar, but the man who is really wealthy is the fellow who still has his first friend.

—Anonymous

Country Sides

Brown Sugar Beans

Lisa Sabula
Ostrander, OH

An old-fashioned favorite our family loves.

1/4 c. onion, chopped
4 slices bacon, cut in pieces
1/2 c. catsup

1/4 c. brown sugar
1 T. Worcestershire sauce
15-oz. can green beans, drained

Brown onion and bacon. Add catsup, brown sugar and Worcestershire sauce. Simmer 2 minutes. Place green beans in one-quart casserole dish. Pour sauce over beans. Do not stir. Bake at 350 degrees for 20 minutes.

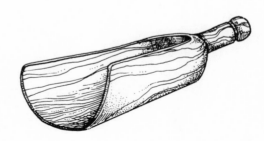

Paint and sand the edges of small mismatched drawers. Stack and fill with potpourri, rosehips, star anise or cinnamon sticks.

Grandma Leland's Red Cabbage

Suzan Detwiler
Easton, PA

Our family especially likes this dish ...
it brings back some wonderful memories.

1 head of red cabbage
3 T. shortening
1 onion, sliced
1/2 t. whole cloves

1 c. white vinegar
3 c. water
sugar to taste

Shred cabbage and sauté in shortening. Add onion. Add cloves, vinegar, and water. Let boil, cover and let simmer for approximately one hour. When cooled, add sugar to taste. Serves 8 to 10.

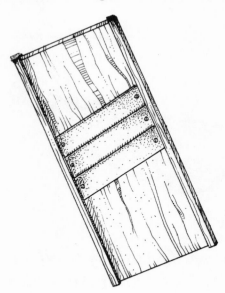

Use a shadowbox to display Grandma's old-fashioned kitchen utensils and her favorite recipe cards.

Pickled Mushrooms

Linda Spain
Ashley, OH

We could always count on Grandma Spain to bring her pickled mushrooms to any family get-together...and they never lasted long! Even though she is no longer with us, we still think of her whenever someone makes this recipe.

1/3 c. red wine vinegar
1/3 c. oil
1 sm. onion, thinly sliced and
    separated into rings
1 t. salt

2 t. dried parsley flakes
1 t. yellow mustard
1 T. brown sugar
3 4-oz. jars button mushrooms

In a small saucepan, combine all ingredients except the mushrooms. When mixture comes to a boil, add mushrooms and simmer for 5 minutes. Pour into a bowl, cover and chill for several hours or overnight, stirring occasionally. Drain before serving.

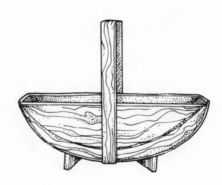

A happy family is but an earlier heaven.

–John Bowring

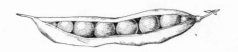

Birch Bayh Green Beans

Margaretta Wilson
Marshall, IL

This recipe is a Wilson family favorite! My mother-in-law copied the recipe out of a 1964 Democratic Cookbook, changing it slightly to suit the tastes of her family. The recipe was named after Birch Bayh, a Senator in Indiana at the time. It was originally submitted to the Democratic cookbook by his wife, who said "my husband prefers this to ice cream!" My mother-in-law has since passed away, but her daughters-in-law and granddaughters have carried on this traditional dish.

2 14-1/4 oz. cans French-style
   green beans
10-3/4 oz. can cream of mushroom or cream of celery soup

8 slices processed cheese
2.8-oz. can French fried
   onion rings

Drain liquid from green beans. Pour one can of beans into a 2-quart casserole dish. On top of beans layer 1/2 can of soup, 4 slices of cheese and 1/2 can of onion rings. Top onion rings with remaining beans, soup and cheese. Bake at 350 degrees for 35 to 45 minutes. Top with remaining onion rings for last 5 minutes of baking.

The greatest essentials of happiness are something to do, someone to love, and something to hope for.

-Anonymous

Marinated Vegetables

Jennifer Woodruff
Van Buren, AR

A favorite at our house! It's requested at every family gathering!

14-1/4 oz. can green peas
14-1/4 oz. can French-style
    green beans

14-1/4 oz. can corn
1 red pepper, chopped
1 sm. red onion, chopped

Drain peas, beans, and corn and place in a large bowl. Add chopped pepper and onion, mix well. Toss with dressing.

Dressing:

1 c. sugar
1 c. water
2/3 c. oil

2/3 c. white vinegar
1 t. salt (optional)

Bring ingredients to a boil. Pour over vegetables. Chill overnight for best results. Should be chilled for at least 4 hours.

Happiness is like a potato salad...when shared with others, it's a picnic!

—Anonymous

Butternut Squash

Dorothy Foor
Jeromesville, OH

The crumb topping adds a special crunch!

1-1/2 lbs. butternut squash,
    peeled and cut into cubes
2 T. all-purpose flour
2 T. lemon juice

1 t. cinnamon
1/4 t. salt
1/3 c. dry bread crumbs
2 T. chicken broth

Heat oven to 350 degrees. Spray an 8"x8" baking dish with non-stick cooking spray. Mix all ingredients except bread crumbs and broth. Spread in pan and bake uncovered for 50 minutes or until squash is tender. Mix bread crumbs and broth. Spread evenly over squash. Set oven control to broil. Broil squash about 4 inches from heat for 3 minutes or until bread crumbs are brown. Serves 6.

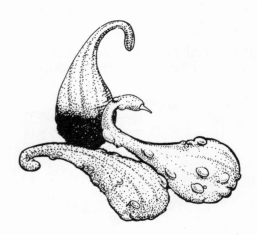

Display your antique pull-toys on a round wooden plant stand.

Country Sides

Garlic Smashed Potatoes

Vickie

A favorite in our house...sprinkle some chives on top for extra flavor!

5 lbs. potatoes, peeled and cubed
1 head garlic
1 T. vegetable oil
1/2 c. butter

8-oz. pkg. cream cheese,
   softened
1 c. sour cream
salt to taste

Place potatoes in a Dutch oven, cover with water and bring to a boil. Continue to cook until potatoes are tender. Drain and set aside. Cut garlic horizontally and place in a baking dish. Drizzle with oil and bake at 350 degrees for 30 minutes or until tender. Using a fork, remove skin and mash garlic. Mash potatoes, add garlic and remaining ingredients; blend well. Spoon potatoes into a 13"x9" baking dish. Cover and refrigerate overnight. When ready to serve, heat oven to 350 degrees and bake for 50 to 60 minutes.

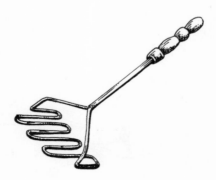

Pray for peace and grace and spiritual food; for wisdom and guidance, for all these are good, but don't forget the potatoes!

-John Tyler Pette

Zesty Broccoli

Barbara Arnold
Toledo, OH

A touch of horseradish makes this creamy broccoli dish even better!

2 10-oz. pkgs. broccoli, chopped
10-3/4 oz. can cream of
   mushroom soup
1-1/2 c. Cheddar cheese,
   shredded
1 egg, beaten

1/4 c. milk
1/4 c. mayonnaise
1 T. horseradish
2 T. butter, melted
1/4 c. cracker crumbs, crushed

Cook broccoli according to package instructions; drain. Combine soup, cheese, egg, milk and mayonnaise. Add horseradish. Stir into broccoli. Spoon into greased 2-quart casserole. Combine butter and crumbs and sprinkle on top. Bake at 350 degrees for 45 minutes.

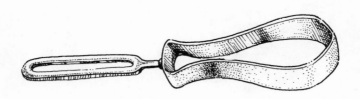

Tuck a votive inside a collection of aged tin or spatterware cups, surround it with rosehips.

Mom's Perky Pickles

Leekay Bennett
Delaware, OH

This recipe is at least 40 years old. As a child, Mom and I would make these together about every other month. She would cut the pickles, I'd add the sugar and pour the juice back into the jar, then Mom would shake the jar...it gave us quiet time together. The name came about when I bit into my first pickle, puckered up, and announced to my grandmother and mom, "These sure are perky pickles!"

2 qts. whole Kosher dill pickles   2 c. sugar

Pour off the juice from the dill pickles and save. Cut pickles 1/2 to 1-1/2 inches thick. Fill jar with a layer of cut pickles, topped with 1/3 cup sugar. Continue layering until jar is firmly packed. Pour the reserved pickle juice back into the jar and seal tightly; shake to distribute sugar. Refrigerate pickles for 4 to 7 days. Shake the jar once a day to make sure the sugar fully dissolves.

You've got to get up every morning with a smile on your face, and show the world all the love in your heart.

-Carole King

Glorified Rice

Donna Cozzens
Laramie, WY

This is a special recipe we always enjoyed with our meal. I can still picture my grandmother arriving for a visit. As soon as her car pulled in to the yard, we would rush out to help her carry the bundles of goodies into our house. Our favorite dishes still warm from her oven; the food was always in the original cooking pots, so as not to lose any flavor. Each dish was wrapped up in a white kitchen dish towel with a tidy knot and handle at the top for carrying. When all of the towels were unfolded we would eagerly gather for dinner. Even though Grandma had transported dinner from her kitchen over the miles to our home, we loved the idea she provided for us...the comforting feeling that we were visiting Grandma's home.

1 c. rice	1-3/4 c. milk
16-oz. can crushed pineapple in heavy syrup, drained	2 T. sugar
	1 c. whipped cream
3-oz. pkg. vanilla pudding	Garnish: maraschino cherries

Boil one cup of rice. Drain and cool. Drain pineapple and add it to the rice. Combine pudding and milk. Mixture should be thick, not thin. Add sugar and chill. Mix pudding, rice and pineapple together. Spread in a 9"x9" serving dish. Spread the top with one cup of whipped cream and decorate to your liking with maraschino cherries.

The world is your cow, but you must milk it.

−Vermont saying

Corn & Tomatoes

LaRayne Cummons
Lakeview, OH

Just-picked vegetables from your garden or the farmers' market make this side dish perfect for a warm weather family picnic!

6 lg. tomatoes
2 c. fresh corn
1/2 t. salt

1/2 t. pepper
1 t. chives, chopped
1/4 t. dried basil

Pour boiling water over tomatoes. Cool slightly. Slip off tomato skins and chop tomatoes. Combine corn and tomatoes in a saucepan. Add salt, pepper, chives and basil. Simmer over low heat for 20 minutes or until vegetables are tender. Serves 6.

An aged wooden checkerboard hung on the wall is perfect for displaying dried flowers or herbs on old tin hooks.

Whipped Sweet Potatoes

Betty Stout
Worthington, OH

Good with lots of melting butter on top!

3 lbs. sweet potatoes, peeled and
    cut into 1-inch pieces
4 carrots, peeled and cut into
    1-inch pieces
2 chicken bouillon cubes
6 T. unsalted butter

1/4 c. light brown sugar, firmly
    packed
2 T. fresh orange juice
1 T. nutmeg, ground
salt, to taste

Place the sweet potatoes, carrots and bouillon cubes in a large heavy pot and cover with cold water. Bring to a boil. Reduce the heat and simmer until the vegetables are very tender, 15 to 20 minutes. Drain, reserving 6 tablespoons of the cooking liquid and place in a bowl. Using a mixer, whip the vegetables with the reserved cooking liquid and the remaining ingredients. Serve immediately or place, covered in a 350 degree oven for 15 to 20 minutes. Serves 6 to 8.

Oh, potatoes, they grow small, for they plant them in the fall and they eat 'em skins and all, in Kansas.

—Kansas song

Grandma's Baked Goods

While growing up, the hot summer days were offset by the fun of enjoying homemade ice cream! Mom would pour a mixture of fresh cream, sugar and milk into our wooden ice cream maker, pack it with ice and salt, secure the lid, and the cranking began!

At first it was easy to crank the handle, even the littlest one could easily do it; however, the job became more difficult as the ice cream hardened. Dad would always have to finish the last few turns, just for good measure! When he removed the lid, there was a crowd of children wanting to lick the dasher after it was removed from the bucket! Growing up, there was nothing like fresh, homemade ice cream on a hot summer day.

After our homemade treat, we would take turns in the simple tree swing, tyring to touch the sky with our toes! Mom would settle in a hammock, fanning herself with a brimmed straw hat.

Grandma's Baked Goods

Honey Bun Cake

Carol Lankford
Danville, VA

Our family loves this cake!

1 box yellow cake mix
4 eggs, beaten
3/4 c. oil
1 c. buttermilk

1 c. brown sugar
2 t. cinnamon
1/2 c. pecans

Mix first 4 ingredients well. Pour into a greased 13"x9" baking dish. Combine brown sugar, cinnamon, and pecans. Swirl into batter. Bake at 300 degrees for 40 to 60 minutes. Check after 40 minutes with a toothpick.

Glaze:

1 c. powdered sugar
2 T. milk

1 t. vanilla

Mix all ingredients together and pour over warm cake.

Old twigs tied together can make a primitive frame for your sampler.

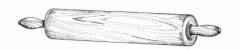

Sour Cream Apple Squares

Pat Habiger
Spearville, KS

Just like apple pie!

2 c. flour
2 c. brown sugar, packed
1/2 c. margarine, softened
1/2 c. nuts, chopped
2 t. cinnamon
1 t. baking soda

1/2 t. salt
1 c. sour cream
1 t. vanilla
1 egg, beaten
2 c. apples, chopped and peeled
Garnish: whipped cream

In a mixing bowl, combine flour, brown sugar, and margarine; blend at low speed until crumbly. Stir in the nuts. Press about 2-3/4 cups of crumb mixture into the bottom of an ungreased 13"x9" pan. To the remaining crumb mixture, add cinnamon baking soda, salt, sour cream, vanilla and egg. Beat until thoroughly combined. Stir in apples. Spoon evenly over bottom layer. Bake at 350 degrees for 35 to 40 minutes. Cool on wire rack. Cut into squares. Garnish with whipped cream. Serves 12 to 15.

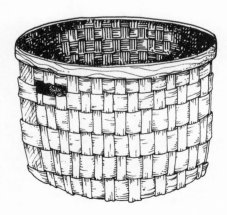

An apple pie without some cheese is like a kiss without a squeeze.

-English proverb

Mystery Pecan Pie

Valeri McCown
Auberry, CA

The mystery is how the layers reverse positions while baking!
Everyone who tastes this pie will want the recipe!

8–oz. pkg. cream cheese
1/3 plus 1/4 cup sugar, divided
1/4 t. salt
2 t. vanilla, separated
4 eggs

1-1/4 c. pecans, chopped
1 c. light corn syrup
1 unbaked pie crust
whipped cream

Preheat oven to 375 degrees. Beat together cream cheese, 1/3 cup sugar, salt, one teaspoon vanilla and one egg. Pour into pie crust. Sprinkle pecans over cream cheese layer. Beat together: 3 eggs, 1/4 cup sugar, one teaspoon vanilla and corn syrup. Pour this mixture over the pecan layer. Bake for 35 to 40 minutes, until filling is firm. Refrigerate before serving. Top with whipped cream. Serves 6 to 8.

Old-fashioned canning jars are great for storing cookie cutters!

Oatmeal Cake

Teresa Cates
Odessa, TX

I remember this recipe as a dessert that my mother prepared on many occasions. Everyone would always compliment her, and now that I'm continuing the tradition, I'm the one getting the compliments... but I owe it all to her.

1 c. oatmeal	2 eggs
1-1/2 c. boiling water	1/8 t. salt
1/2 c. butter	1-1/2 c. flour
1 c. sugar	1 t. baking soda
1 c. brown sugar	1 t. cinnamon

Mix oatmeal and boiling water. Let stand for 20 minutes. Cream butter and sugars together. Add eggs and salt, combine with oatmeal. Stir in flour, soda and cinnamon. Bake in a greased and floured 13"x9" pan at 325 degrees for 35 minutes.

Icing:

3/4 c. butter	1 c. pecans
1 c. brown sugar	2 c. coconut
1/2 c. half-and-half	

Mix all ingredients together and spoon over warm cake. Place under broiler until bubbly.

Hold a true friend with both thy hands.

-Nigerian Proverb

Fudgy-Topped Brownies

Carole Foltman
Williams Bay, WI

These truly satisfy a chocolate craving!

1/2 c. butter
1 c. sugar
4 eggs, beaten
1 c. flour

16–oz. can chocolate syrup
1 t. vanilla
1 c. nuts, chopped

Cream together butter and sugar. Add eggs, flour, chocolate syrup, vanilla and nuts. Bake at 350 degrees in a 13"x9" pan for 40 minutes or a 15"x10" jelly roll pan for 20 minutes. Frost while warm.

Frosting:

1-1/3 c. sugar
6 T. butter

6 T. milk
6–oz pkg. chocolate chips

Combine sugar, butter and milk in a saucepan; stir until completely dissolved. Bring to a boil for one minute. Remove from heat and add chocolate chips. Mix quickly until chips dissolve, spread over warm brownies.

A copper boiler filled with kindling, gives a feeling of grandma's kitchen when set next to your stove.

Praline-Apple Crisp

Cheryl Bierley
Miamisburg, OH

Serve warm with a little milk poured over top.

1 T. water
1 t. almond extract
6 c. tart apples, sliced
2 T. margarine
2 T. all-purpose flour

2 T. brown sugar, packed
1/2 t. cinnamon, ground
1/2 c. zwieback crackers, crushed
2 T. pecans, chopped

Preheat oven to 375 degrees. Spray 1-1/2 quart casserole with non-stick cooking spray. Mix water and almond extract, toss with apples in casserole. Cut margarine into flour, brown sugar and cinnamon with pastry blender in small bowl until mixture is crumbly. Stir in crackers and pecans. Sprinkle over apples. Bake uncovered about 30 minutes or until top is golden brown and apples are tender. Serve warm. Serves 6.

Old quilt rag balls look wonderful spilling from a gathering basket! Display them on your step-back cupboard or on a dry sink.

Blackberry Cobbler

Judy Cheatham
Brentwood, TN

This cobbler is so delicious...the crust rises to the surface!
We love it served with a big scoop of vanilla ice cream!

1/2 c. butter
1 c. flour
2 c. sugar
1 t. baking powder

1/2 t. nutmeg
1/2 c. half-and-half
1 t. vanilla
2 c. blackberries

Preheat oven to 350 degrees. Melt the butter in a square 9" baking dish in the oven. In a medium bowl, whisk together the flour, one cup sugar, baking powder and nutmeg. Combine the half-and-half and vanilla in a measuring cup, then add to the flour mixture blending until crumbly. Press the dough into the baking dish on top of the butter, some butter will spill over on the dough. In a medium saucepan, stir together the berries with the remaining one cup of sugar. Warm over low heat and pour over the dough. Bake for 50 to 55 minutes or until the crust is golden brown.

A milkman's old-fashioned bottle carrier makes a wonderful picnic basket! Fill it with lunch, canning jars full of icy lemonade and tie a bandanna napkin on the handle!

Strawberry Shortcake

Terri Harkins
Philadelphia, PA

When my grandmother wrote this recipe down, everything was a pinch of this and a dash of that. I remember it because my grandmother was the best cook! I will always remember the smell of her kitchen, and this recipe brings her closer to me.

2 eggs
1 c. sugar
1 t. vanilla
1 c. flour
1 t. baking powder

1/2 c. milk
3 T. butter
1 pt. heavy cream, whipped
2 c. strawberries, sliced
powdered sugar to taste

Beat eggs and sugar together. Continue beating and add vanilla. Combine flour and baking powder; add to the egg and sugar mixture. Heat milk and butter, then add to mixture. Grease and flour a 9"x8" pan, pour in mixture. Bake at 350 degrees for 20 minutes. This makes one layer. For 2 layers repeat recipe. Cool cake. Spread cake with whipped cream, sliced strawberries, and sprinkle with powdered sugar when serving.

Build a shelf out of barnsiding or discarded boards, then paint, stain and sand the edges to make it look old. Attach hooks and hang a kitchen collection of enamel cups, a potato masher, sifter, or pastry blender.

Grandma's Baked Goods

German Chocolate Pie

Pauline Raens
Abilene, TX

A quick and easy recipe for family gatherings.

2 1-oz. squares German sweet
   chocolate
1 c. butter
3 eggs
2 T. flour
1 c. sugar

1 t. vanilla
1 c. pecans, chopped
1/2 c. coconut
Garnish: whipped cream, shaved
   chocolate and pecans

Melt chocolate and butter over low heat and let cool. Beat eggs, flour, sugar and vanilla together for 3 minutes at high speed. Pour chocolate mixture over eggs and beat 3 more minutes.
Add pecans and coconut. Pour into well buttered 9" pie plate. Bake at 350 degrees for 28 minutes. Cool just before serving. Top with whipped cream and garnish with shaved chocolate and pecans. Serves 6.

I always have a chair for you in the smallest parlor in the world, to wit, my heart.

-Emily Dickinson

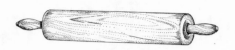

Warm Turtle Cake

Laurie Benham
Playas, New Mexico

A cake that reminds me of the boxes of chocolate-covered turtles that my dad used to bring home for us when we were little!

1 box Swiss chocolate cake mix
1/3 c. plus 1/2 c. evaporated
   milk, divided
3/4 c. butter, melted

14-oz. pkg. caramels
1 c. pecan pieces
3/4 c. chocolate chips

Blend together cake mix, 1/3 cup evaporated milk and melted butter on medium speed for 2 minutes. Pour half of mixture into a greased 11"x7" cake pan. Bake at 350 degrees for 6 minutes. In a double boiler or microwave, melt 1/2 cup evaporated milk and caramels. Drizzle over cake. Sprinkle pecan pieces and chocolate chips over caramels. Use a wet knife to spread the remaining cake mixture over the pecan pieces and chocolate chips. Bake at 350 degrees for 18 minutes. Serves 12.

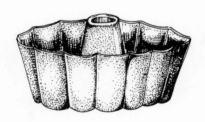

Create your own seasoning mixes from herbs in your garden! For gift-giving, tuck them inside plastic-lined homespun bags tied with raffia!

Grandma's Baked Goods

Grandma Eddy's Apple Crumble

Mary Warren
Auburn, MI

An old family favorite that brings back memories of our visits to my husband's mother's and grandmother's homes. There was always a dish of apple, cherry, blueberry or blackberry crumble around whenever we stopped to visit. When my children were small I started making this family recipe and now my daughter and son help carry on the family tradition.

3/4 c. margarine, softened
3/4 c. flour
3/4 c. brown sugar
3/4 c. quick oats
1/8 t. salt

4 to 6 apples, peeled, cored and
    sliced
cinnamon to taste
1/4 c. sugar

Mix first 5 ingredients until crumbly, set side. Place apples in a 13"x9" pan; sprinkle with cinnamon and sugar. Place brown sugar topping over all and bake at 375 degrees for 30 minutes, or until topping is lightly browned and crunchy.

If you have built castles in the air, your work need not be lost; that is where they should be. Now put foundations under them.

—Henry David Thoreau

Peanut Butter Pie

Deb Robb
Lucas, IA

Chocolate and peanut butter...perfect together!

8 oz. cream cheese
1 c. sugar
1 c. chunky peanut butter
1 t. vanilla
2 T. butter, melted

12 oz. frozen whipped topping, divided
1 chocolate cookie pie crust
2 T. chocolate ice cream topping, warmed

Soften cream cheese to room temperature. Cream with sugar, peanut butter and vanilla. Mix well. Add melted butter. Fold in frozen whipped topping, reserving one cup. Pour into prepared crust. Drizzle top of pie with the chocolate ice cream topping. Serve with reserved frozen whipped topping.

Chocolate Cookie Crust:

1-1/2 c. chocolate sandwich cookies, crushed fine

6 T. butter, melted

Mix cookies with butter and firmly press into 9" pie plate. Chill until ready to use.

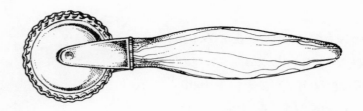

A friend is a present which you give yourself.

-Robert Louis Stevenson

Grandma's Baked Goods

Molasses Sugar Cookies

Mary Sewell
Milford, CT

When I bake these cookies the smell reminds me of when my children were little. When they came home from school and realized I'd made them, they would jump for joy!

3/4 c. shortening
1 c. sugar
1/4 c. molasses
1 egg
2 c. flour

2 t. baking soda
1/2 t. ground cloves
1/2 t. ginger
1 t. cinnamon
1/2 t. salt

Melt shortening and cool. Add sugar, molasses and egg. Beat well. Sift together flour, baking soda, spices and salt. Combine with mixture. Mix and chill for 4 hours. Form in one-inch balls and roll in granulated sugar. Place on greased cookie sheet. Bake at 375 degrees for 8 to 10 minutes. Cool and enjoy. Makes 50 cookies.

Live decently, fearlessly, joyously and don't forget that in the long run it is not the years in your life but the life in your years that counts!

-Adlai Stevenson

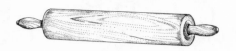

Fresh Peach Pie

Susan Brzozowski
Ellicott City, MD

It's a tradition for my mom and me to make fruit pies when she visits. While making the pies, I have the pleasure of Mom's company as well as her help; then we share this family favorite with my husband and daughter that evening. I freeze a second pie to enjoy the taste and memories when Mom can't be with us.

1 c. sugar
2-1/2 T. cornstarch
1/4 t. salt
1/2 c. water

4 or 5 c. peaches, sliced and peeled
1 T. lemon juice

Combine sugar, cornstarch, and salt in a large saucepan. Add water and peaches. Bring to a boil and boil for one minute, stirring constantly. Cool on a rack; then add lemon juice. Pour the cooled peach mixture into a pastry-lined 9" pie crust. Roll the remaining pie crust dough and fit over top. Seal the edges well and cut vents in top. Bake on lower shelf of oven at 425 degrees for 50 minutes. If desired, brush milk on top of crust to aid in browning.

Standard Pie Crust:

2 c. flour, sifted
1 t. salt

3/4 c. shortening
4 T. cold water

Put flour and salt in mixing bowl and mix. Cut in shortening as follows: For a tender crust, cut in about 2/3 of the shortening with pastry blender or 2 knives until as fine as meal. For a flaky crust, cut in the remaining shortening to the size of large peas. Sprinkle all the water, one tablespoon at a time, over different parts of mixture. Mix thoroughly with fork until all particles cling together and form a dough. Using your hands, work crust into a smooth ball. Roll out on a floured board or cloth.

Grandma's Baked Goods

Aunt Esther's Chocolate Chip Cookies

Cindy Caretto
Irvine, CA

Aunt Esther was a wonderful cook. I can't take these cookies anywhere without being asked for the recipe!

1 c. butter, softened
1/4 c. sugar
3/4 c. brown sugar, packed
3-1/2 oz. pkg. vanilla instant
    pudding
1 t. baking soda

1 t. vanilla
2 eggs
2-1/2 c. flour
2 c. chocolate chips
1 c. nuts, optional

Beat together butter, sugar, brown sugar, pudding mix, baking soda and vanilla. Beat in eggs. Add flour and stir together. Stir in chocolate chips and nuts. Drop by heaping teaspoonfuls about 2 inches apart on an ungreased cookie sheet. Bake for 9-1/2 minutes at 375 degrees in a conventional oven or 10 minutes at 325 degrees in a convection oven. Butterscotch or chocolate instant pudding may be substituted for the vanilla pudding. Chocolate candies or butterscotch chips may replace the chocolate chips. Makes 48 cookies.

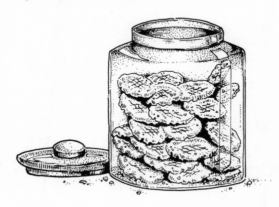

If you would be loved, love and be loveable.

-Benjamin Franklin

Chocolate Mayonnaise Cake

Debby Sprechman
Pembroke Pines, FL

So rich and moist! It always reminds me of our special family visits.

2 c. flour
2 t. baking soda
1-1/4 c. cocoa
1/2 t. salt

1 c. mayonnaise
1 c. sugar
1 c. cold coffee
2 t. vanilla

Combine flour, baking soda, cocoa and salt; set aside. In a bowl, blend mayonnaise and sugar at medium speed. Gradually beat in coffee and vanilla. Add dry ingredients and beat until well blended; batter will be thick. Spread into a greased and floured 11"x7" pan. Bake at 350 degrees for 30 to 35 minutes or until done. Cool and frost.

Frosting:

2 T. butter
1 c. powdered sugar

1 to 2 t. milk
1 t. vanilla

Blend all ingredients together, adjusting milk until the desired consistency is achieved.

Attach a wooden board to the top of an old window frame. Add little wire hooks to the front edge of the shelf to hold a collection of old-fashioned kitchen utensils.

Grandma's Baked Goods

Old-Fashioned Raspberry Cutouts

Rebecca LaDue
Oshkosh, WI

These cookies represent many happy memories of special past occasions. The recipe is over 90 years old, given to my mother by an elderly neighbor who was like a grandmother to me.

1 c. butter, room temperature
1/2 c. sugar
1 c. walnuts, finely chopped

2 c. flour
raspberry jam

Cream the butter and sugar. Chop the walnuts in a food processor or blender to nearly a paste consistency. Blend in flour and chopped walnuts to butter mixture. Roll out onto a floured surface and cut into your favorite shapes. Bake at 350 degrees on ungreased cookie sheets for 10 minutes. Be careful not to overbake, cookies should be soft. When warm, roll in sugar and fill with jam, pressing 2 cookies gently together. Makes 2 to 3 dozen cookies depending on size of your cookie cutter.

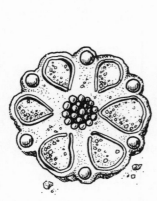

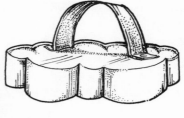

If the world seems cold to you, kindle fires to warm it.

—Lucy Larcom

Apple Dumplings

Kathy Wheeler
Hillsdale, NY

This recipe was handed down to me from my mother. Many years ago Mom made three recipe books; one for each of her children. She filled the pages with her favorite recipes and some that were handed down from my grandmother. These recipe books were meant to be given to us at Christmas, but two days before Christmas Mom passed away unexpectedly. These books are a treasure...a part of her that we'll always have. This is my favorite recipe from that book.

2 c. flour
4 t. baking powder
1/4 t. salt
2 T. sugar
2 T. shortening

1 c. milk
6 baking apples, peeled and
   chopped
1/2 c. water

Mix first 4 ingredients, blend in shortening with a fork. Add milk gradually and blend with a fork until dough is soft. Set aside. In a heavy saucepan, add apples and enough water to keep apples from sticking while cooking. Cover, bring to a boil and add dumpling dough by spoonfuls on top of apples. Cover, reduce heat to medium and cook 12 to 15 minutes. Uncover saucepan so dumplings don't become soggy.

Vanilla Sauce:

1-1/2 c. water
1 T. lemon zest
1/2 c. sugar
1-1/2 T. cornstarch

1-1/2 t. vanilla
2 T. margarine
1/2 t. cinnamon
1/8 t. nutmeg

Boil water with lemon peel. Mix sugar and cornstarch and add to water stirring constantly and cook until thickened. Remove from heat. Add vanilla, margarine, cinnamon and nutmeg. Serve over dumplings. Serves 6.

Grandma's Baked Goods

Grandma Runkle's Sugar Cakes

Julie Bell
New Market, VA

This recipe belonged to my great-grandmother. I remember it well because no one would make these sugar cakes like Grandma Runkle! When I was growing up, I spent Saturday mornings with my great-grandparents and the first thing I would be asked when I arrived was, "Julia, would you like something to eat? I have sugar cakes!" They were the best!

2 c. granulated sugar
1 c. butter or margarine
3 eggs, beaten
2 t. baking soda

1 c. buttermilk
1 t. baking powder
4 c. flour
1/2 t. salt

Lightly oil a cookie sheet and set aside. Mix sugar and butter. Add eggs and beat well. Put baking soda in buttermilk. Sift baking powder with flour and salt. Add flour and milk alternately. Pour batter onto cookie sheet in the size of a silver dollar and bake at 350 degrees for 10 minutes.

Decorate with flea-market finds such as metal basket holders, colorful glasses, or glass drawer pulls...they'll bring back a feeling of comfort from Grandma's house.

Texas Sheet Cake

Jean Shaffer
Washington Court House, OH

Family and friends will look forward to eating this chocolate cake!

2 c. flour
2 c. sugar
1/2 t. salt
1/2 c. shortening
1/2 c. margarine
1 c. water

3 T. cocoa
2 eggs, beaten
1/2 c. buttermilk
1 t. baking soda
1 t. vanilla

In large bowl mix flour, sugar and salt. In saucepan mix together shortening, margarine, water and cocoa. Bring to a boil then mix with dry ingredients. In a small bowl mix eggs, buttermilk, baking soda and vanilla. Add to chocolate mixture. Combine well and pour on a greased and floured cookie sheet. Bake at 350 degrees for 25 minutes. During last 5 minutes of baking, prepare icing.

Icing:

1/2 c. margarine
3 T. cocoa
4 c. powdered sugar

1 t. vanilla
4 T. milk

Melt margarine and cocoa. Then add powdered sugar, vanilla and milk. Stir until smooth. Ice immediately while cake is hot.

The ornaments of a house are the guests who frequent it.

-Anonymous

Grandma's Baked Goods

Raspberry Nut Pinwheels

Pat Habiger
Spearville, KS

Pat won first prize in a holiday baking contest with this recipe!

2 c. flour
1 t. baking powder
1/2 c. margarine, softened
1 c. sugar

1 egg
1 t. vanilla
1/4 c. seedless raspberry jam
1 c. walnuts, finely chopped

Sift together flour and baking powder. Beat together margarine, sugar and egg in large bowl until fluffy. Stir in vanilla. Gradually add flour mixture, stirring until well combined. Roll out dough between 2 pieces of wax paper to 12"x10" rectangle. Remove top piece of wax paper. Spread jam evenly over entire surface of dough. Sprinkle with nuts. Firmly roll up dough from the long side, removing wax paper. Refrigerate several hours or overnight. When ready to make cookies, preheat oven to 375 degrees. Cut roll into generous 1/4-inch slices with a sharp knife. Transfer slices to ungreased cookie sheet, spacing 2 inches apart. Bake in preheated oven for 9 minutes or until golden around edges. Cool on wire racks.

Just the knowledge that a good book is awaiting one at the end of a long day makes that day happier.

–Kathleen Norris

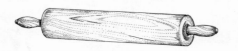

Carrot Cake

Karen Moran
Navasota, TX

I remember my mother baking this for my father's birthday...it was his favorite cake!.

4 eggs, lightly beaten
1-1/2 c. oil
2-1/2 c. sugar
3 c. flour
2 t. baking powder
2 t. baking soda
1 t. salt

2 t. cinnamon
3 c. carrots, grated
15-1/4 oz. can crushed
   pineapple, drained
1-1/2 to 2 c. nuts, chopped
1 t. vanilla

In a large mixing bowl add eggs, oil and sugar, blending well. Add all dry ingredients and stir until smooth. Stir in carrots, pineapple, nuts and vanilla. Pour into 3 greased and floured 9" cake pans. Bake at 350 degrees for 25 to 30 minutes or until done. Cool in pans for 10 minutes. Remove from pans and cool completely.

Frosting:

2 8-oz. pkgs. cream cheese,
   softened
1/2 c. margarine
2 16-oz. pkgs. powdered sugar,
   sifted

2 t. vanilla
1 c. nuts, chopped

Cream together all ingredients and spread between layers and over cooled cake.

A friend may well be reckoned the masterpiece of nature.

-Ralph Waldo Emerson

Grandma's Baked Goods

Chocolate Refrigerator Cookies

Judy Kelly
St. Charles, MO

My mom rarely uses a recipe when she cooks, but she found this one in a cookbook that I gave her 30 years ago and has been making them every since.

1-1/4 c. butter, softened	3 c. cake flour
1-1/2 c. powdered sugar	1/2 c. cocoa
1 egg	1/4 t. salt

Thoroughly mix butter, sugar and egg. Blend in flour, cocoa and salt. Cover and chill for one hour. Divide dough in half. Shape each half into a roll 1-1/2 inches in diameter. Wrap and chill at least 8 hours. Heat oven to 400 degrees. Cut rolls into 1/8-inch slices. If dough crumbles while cutting, let warm slightly. Place one inch apart on ungreased baking sheet. Bake about 8 minutes. Immediately remove from baking sheet and cool. Frost with fudge frosting. Makes 8 dozen cookies.

Fudge Frosting:

1/4 c. shortening	1/4 t. salt
1/3 c. milk	1 t. vanilla
1 c. sugar	
2 oz. unsweetened chocolate, melted	

Bring all ingredients except vanilla to a rolling boil, stirring occasionally. Boil one minute without stirring. Place pan in bowl of ice and water. Beat until frosting is thick and cold. Stir in vanilla.

Dutch Apple Cake

Neta Liebscher
El Reno, OK

When our apples are ripe on the tree in the front yard, it's time to bake a family favorite!

1/2 c. shortening
1/2 c. brown sugar, packed
1 egg
1/4 c. milk
1 c. flour

1 t. baking powder
1/2 t. cinnamon
1 c. Cheddar cheese, shredded
   and divided

Cream together shortening, brown sugar and egg. Add milk, flour, baking powder and cinnamon. Stir in 1/2 of Cheddar cheese. Pour mixture into a greased and floured Bundt® pan.

Topping:

3-1/2 c. apples, peeled and
   chopped
1 t. cinnamon

1/2 c. sugar
1/2 c. nuts, chopped

Mix together apples, cinnamon, sugar and nuts. Put mixture on top of cake in Bundt® pan. Bake at 325 degrees for 30 minutes. Top with 1/2 cup Cheddar cheese while still hot. Let cool then remove from pan and serve.

A house is a home when it shelters the body and comforts the soul.

-Phillip Moffitt

Grandma's Baked Goods

Sherry's Spicy Cutouts

Terri Vanden Bosch
Rock Valley, IA

This recipe was given to me by a dear friend and since then it's become a favorite at our house!

1 c. margarine
1 c. sugar
1/2 c. brown sugar, packed
1 egg
1/4 c. molasses
1 t. salt
1 t. baking soda

1/2 t. baking powder
1 t. cinnamon
1/2 t. ginger
1/2 t. nutmeg
3 c. flour
1 c. quick cooking oatmeal

Cream margarine and sugars. Add egg and molasses and beat until fluffy. Sift together dry ingredients and add gradually to creamed mixture. Stir in oatmeal. Roll out to 1/8-inch thickness on a board sprinkled with powdered sugar. Cut out with cookie cutters. Bake at 350 degrees on a slightly greased cookie sheet for 7 to 10 minutes. Cool one minute before removing. Frost as desired.

Jump into the middle of things, get your hands dirty, fall flat on your face, and then reach for the stars!

-Joan L. Curcio

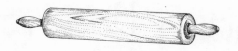

Raisin Crumb Bars

Judy Kelly
St. Charles, MO

This is an old family recipe that makes a tasty dessert.

2 c. raisins
1 c. brown sugar
1 c. butter
1-3/4 c. quick cooking oatmeal
1-3/4 c. flour
1 t. baking soda
1/2 c. nuts, chopped

3 egg yolks
1-1/2 c. sour cream
1 c. sugar
1/4 t. salt
3 T. cornstarch
1 t. cinnamon

Boil raisins in small amount of water until plump. Drain. Combine brown sugar, butter, oatmeal, flour, baking soda and nuts. Press half of mixture into 13"x9" pan and bake at 350 degrees for 10 minutes. Beat together egg yolks and sour cream. Mix remaining dry ingredients and add to egg mixture. Cook until thickened. Add raisins. Pour over crust and sprinkle with remaining crumbs. Bake at 350 degrees for 30 minutes.

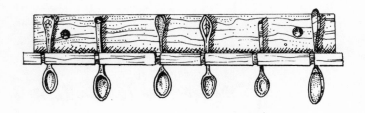

Don't hurry, don't worry.
You're only here for a short visit.
So be sure to stop and smell the flowers.

-Walter Hagen

Sour Cream Pound Cake

Jill Henson
Spruce Pine, NC

When I was young, every Friday and Saturday night we had this wonderful, rich, moist cake! It was a treat I always looked forward to.

1 c. butter	1/4 t. baking soda
3 c. sugar	1/2 pt. sour cream
6 eggs	1 t. vanilla
3 c. flour, sifted	

Cream butter well; gradually add sugar, cream again. Add eggs, one at a time, beating well after each. Sift together flour and baking soda. Gradually add to butter mixture, alternating with sour cream. Add vanilla. Pour into an oiled tube or Bundt® pan. Bake at 325 degrees for 1-1/2 hours. Test for doneness with a toothpick. Let cake cool in pan for 5 minutes, gently remove.

Oh, cakes and friends we should choose with care, not always the fanciest cake that's there is the best to eat! And the plainest friend is sometimes the finest one in the end!

—Margaret Sangster

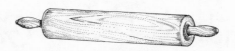

Ice Box Brownies

Tami Bowman
Gooseberry Patch

A chewy brownie that's almost like eating fudge...wonderful!

1/4 c. butter
1-1/2 sq. unsweetened chocolate
1 egg, beaten
1 c. brown sugar, packed
1/2 c. flour

1/4 t. baking powder
1/4 t. salt
1/4 t. vanilla
1/2 c. walnuts, chopped

Melt the butter and chocolate over low heat. Using a mixer, blend the egg, brown sugar and the butter-chocolate mixture for 2 minutes. Sift the flour, baking powder and salt into the mixture. Add the vanilla and beat at medium speed for another minute. Stir in walnuts. Pour into greased 8"x8" pan and bake at 350 degrees for 15 to 18 minutes (325 degrees for glass pan). Remove from oven and allow to cool.

Mint Filling:

1/4 c. butter, softened
1/2 t. vanilla
3/4 t. peppermint extract

2 c. powdered sugar
2 T. milk
few drops green food coloring

In a small bowl, beat all ingredients for 2 to 3 minutes until smooth. Let stand in refrigerator until fairly cold and thick, about 1/2 hour. Spread over cooked brownie cake. Chill for an additional 1/2 hour in refrigerator. Spread with glaze, cut into squares and store in refrigerator.

Glaze:

2 sq. unsweetened chocolate   1 T. butter

Melt chocolate and butter over low heat. Pour over filling and spread.

Peach-Berry Cobbler

Pam Schreiber
Waco, TX

This cobbler is so yummy topped with whipped cream!

1 box yellow cake mix
1/2 t. cinnamon
1/4 t. nutmeg
1 c. margarine or butter,
    softened
1/2 c. nuts, chopped

21-oz. can peach pie filling
16-oz. can whole cranberry
    sauce
vanilla ice cream or whipped
    topping

Preheat oven to 350 degrees. Combine dry cake mix, cinnamon and nutmeg in bowl. Cut in butter with pastry blender until crumbly. Stir in nuts and set aside. Combine peach pie filling and cranberry sauce in ungreased 13"x9" pan. Mix well. Sprinkle crumb mixture over the fruit. Bake at 350 degrees for 45 to 50 minutes or until golden brown. Serve warm with ice cream or whipped topping. Serves 16.

She knew what all smart women knew: Laughter made you live better and longer.

-Gail Parent

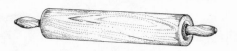

Mom's Apple Crisp

Joan Belitsky
Reading, PA

We had a couple of apple trees at my wonderful childhood home and on the weekends my father would pick the ripe apples and bring them inside. I can remember many a Sunday afternoon, when dusk was beginning to fall, walking through the front door, into our warm home, and smelling Mom's apple crisp. It was a nice way to end the weekend. Now I make it for my own family.

3 or 4 lg. cooking apples, sliced
   and peeled
1/2 c. butter
3/4 c. brown sugar, packed

3/4 c. quick cooking oats
1/2 c. flour
1 t. cinnamon

Arrange apples in 8"x8" square baking dish. Melt butter in saucepan, stir in other ingredients until crumbly. Spread over apples. Bake in 350 degree oven for 35 minutes or until apples are soft. Serves 4 to 6.

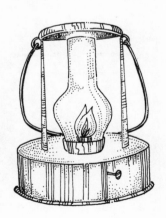

Good friends, good books, and a sleepy conscience: this is the ideal life.

-Mark Twain

Grandma's Baked Goods

Peanut Butter Fudge

Judy Kelly
St. Charles, MO

This is easy to make and so creamy! A great gift for friends.

4-1/2 c. sugar
1-2/3 c. evaporated milk
1/2 c. butter
2 c. crunchy peanut butter

1 c. creamy peanut butter
8 oz. marshmallow cream
2 t. vanilla

Bring sugar, milk and butter to a boil over medium heat for 8 minutes, stirring constantly; remove from heat and stir in peanut butter, marshmallow cream and vanilla. Pour into buttered 13"x9" pan. Let cool in pan. Cut into squares, wrap individually and box for gifts or store and cut as needed.

Grandma's sewing box looks best left open to view the inside...mismatched buttons, pin cushions, colorful spools of thread and thimbles; all bring back warm memories.

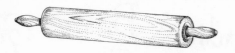

Apple Brown Betty

Tina Stidam
Ashley, OH

Some of my fondest memories are from when I was a little girl spending time with my grandparents. Every Sunday, Granny would fix a feast when the family gathered together. This recipe is one of many I absolutely loved! Grandpa and I would make homemade ice cream to top our dessert. It's a wonderful recipe...I can still smell the aroma in the air.

8 slices white bread, torn
1/2 c. butter, melted
1 t. cinnamon
2-1/2 lbs. Granny Smith apples,
    peeled, cored and sliced

2/3 c. light brown sugar, packed
2 T. lemon juice
1 t. vanilla extract
1/4 t. nutmeg

Preheat oven to 400 degrees. In a 15-1/2"x10-1/2" jelly roll pan, bake bread slices until very lightly toasted; about 15 minutes. Stir occasionally. Grease a 2-quart baking dish, set aside. In a medium bowl, combine butter, 1/2 teaspoon cinnamon and bread, toss gently until evenly moistened. In a large mixing bowl, toss sliced apples, brown sugar, lemon juice, vanilla, nutmeg and remaining cinnamon. Place 1/2 cup bread in baking dish, top with half the apple mixture. Layer with one cup bread pieces and remaining apple mixture. Toss remaining bread over apple mixture, leaving a one-inch border around the edge. Cover with foil and bake for 40 minutes, Uncover and bake 10 minutes longer. Let stand 10 minutes before serving. Serves 8.

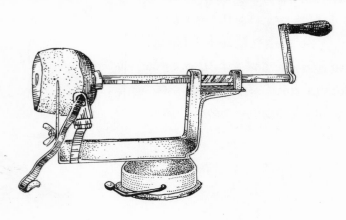

Grandma's Baked Goods

Daisy Brown Sugar Cookies

Kathy Rusert
Mena, AR

My German grandmother kept this cookie dough in the refrigerator so that whenever we came to visit, she always had fresh cookies for us!

2 c. brown sugar
1 c. shortening
2 eggs
3 c. flour

1 t. baking soda
1 t. baking powder
1 t. vanilla
1/2 c. pecans, chopped

Mix brown sugar, shortening and eggs. Cream well. Add remaining ingredients, mixing well. Roll into 2, 2-inch wide rolls; slice and bake at 375 degrees for 8 minutes.

A grandmother is a person with too much wisdom to let that stop her from making a fool of herself over her grandchildren!

-Phil Moss

Index

Index

Turnip Casserole

2 lbs turnip cubed water to cover
1/2 cup soft bread crumbs.
2 tbsps melted butter
1 cup milk
1 tsp salt
1/2 tsp nutmeg
Pepper to taste
1 tbsp sugar
2 eggs lightly beaten

Cook turnip Drain & mash.
Blend remaining ingredients
Turn in buttered dish 1/2 qt.
Bake 350 F for 45 Min

Rice & Carrot Casserole

1/2 cup short grain rice
1 cup water
1 1/4 cup milk
1 lb carrots
1 tbsp melted butter
2 tsp salt
2 tsp sugar
1 Egg.

Cook Rice Cover set aside until this
add grated carrots melted butter salt sugar
& egg Pour into greased casserole
Dot with butter
Bake 350 F 30 45 Min

We've cooked up a whole collection of Gooseberry Patch® books!

Have a taste for more? Call us toll-free at
1-800-854-6673

We'll send you our latest catalog filled with snowmen, Santas, ornaments, candles, cookie cutters, gourmet goodies, salt-glazed pottery collectibles and MORE...including our best-selling cookbooks!

Phone us:
1·800·854·6673

Fax us:
1·740·363·7225

Visit our website:
www.gooseberrypatch.com

Send us your favorite recipe!

and the memory that makes it special for you!* We're putting together a brand new **Gooseberry Patch** cookbook, and you're invited to participate. If we select your recipe, your name will appear right along with it...and you'll receive a FREE copy of the book! Mail to:

Vickie & Jo Ann
Gooseberry Patch, Dept. BOOK
P.O. Box 190
Delaware, Ohio 43015

*Please help us by including the number of servings and all other necessary information!

Chicken & Broccoli Casserole

3 cups hot cooked florets
2 cups cubed cooked chicken breast
1 can low fat Broccoli soup
1/3 cup milk
1/2 cup shredded Cheddar cheese
2 T dry bread crumbs
1 t butter or marg melted

Arrange broccoli & chicken in 1.5 qt dish
Pour mixture of soup & milk over
Sprinkle with cheese Top with crumbs
& butter
Bake 425 - 25 min